C000265336

Overtaken by a Butterfly:
40 Years of Running into Trouble
by
Nick Eades
ISBN: 978-1-914933-53-0

Copyright 2023 All rights reserved. No part of this publication may be reproduced, stored in a retrieval system or transmitted in any form or by any means, electronic, mechanical, photocopy, recording org otherwise, without prior written consent of the copyright owner. Nor can it be circulated in any form of binding or cover other than that in which it is published and without similar conditions including this condition being imposed on a subsequent purchaser.

The right of Nick Eades to be identified as the author of this work has been asserted in accordance with the Copyright Designs and Patents Act 1988.

A copy of this book is deposited with the British Library.

Published By: -

i2i

PUBLISHING

i2i Publishing. Manchester.
www.i2i.publishing.co.uk

This book is dedicated to Alfie Eades

Alfie was the most special dog I have ever met. He was my running partner for over a decade. Not once in all those years did he put a paw wrong. From the moment we first met him to the moment we lost him, Alfie brought us joy and a deep sense of unconditional love.

Apart from being a perfect running partner, Alfie was always next to me whenever I sat down to write my books. As soon as he saw me with pen in hand, he would follow me to wherever I had decided to sit. Alfie would then lie on the floor with his head on my feet. When he was tired of that, he would sit next to me and put his head on my lap. He never left my side until I had finished writing for the day. I wrote my first two books literally with Alfie at my side.

In May this year, Alfie left us. We were not there to hold his paw or stroke his head. We cried for weeks. Occasionally, we still find a tennis ball or a lost dog toy and the tears once again start to flow. We miss him that much.

I was halfway through writing this book when he passed away. It took me five months to gather the strength to resume writing without Alf beside me. My publisher, Lionel Ross, has been very accommodating about the delay in the publication of this book. I apologise to those who were expecting an earlier publication date.

Even now, I can feel a little pressure on my toes or my lap as I write. Occasionally, it has not been easy to focus when the tears start again. Alfie's presence is still with us; we know he will always be safe in our hearts.

Sleep well, my dearest friend.

Contents

8

Prologue

The One Race I Could Not Win

It was a beautiful, late autumnal morning. The sun struggled to make its presence felt as the early morning mists clung stubbornly to the cold landscape. I was running up a steep incline, a track I had always referred to as heartbreak hill. I put my head down and pushed through the last, most punishing and gruelling curve. I began to feel all of my sixty-five years of age. Gritting my teeth and hoping that my second, or was it fifth wind would soon kick in, I continued the climb, each step more tortuous than the last. Finally, I could see the brow of the hill and temporary salvation. Relieved that I was now on the final few kilometres, the track that would lead me back to my car was now mainly flat. I felt the usual rush of endorphins as I settled down to enjoy the view from my elevated position. I was in a reflective mood as I marvelled at the panoramic view of the 'Sussex Serengeti' to my right.

The sun had finally won its battle with the early morning mist and was casting my shadow on the road beside me. My mind wandered back to my early running days. It suddenly dawned on me that the shadow that had followed me through past decades bore little resemblance to the rounded image cast to my left. Old age, something I had been desperately trying to run away from, was finally catching up with me. I realised that my pace was almost sedate. I was running well within my comfort zone; no wonder my shadow had grown substantially. I believed that I was still fit. I still ran almost every day. I had a mere kilometre left, a distance I could surely cover with a sprint. With a renewed determination, I increased my pace to a level I had not attempted for a number of years. I felt the wind in my face, as the years slipped away. I was still young; dammit, I could still run as fast as I had done in my youth. The sun shone, and the world looked a much better place. I felt a renewed adrenaline rush as I covered the last few metres. I felt invincible. I was right, and I was still young. Maybe, that shadow I had seen earlier was just a distortion, a trick of the early morning light. And then, just as I reached my fastest pace, a butterfly overtook me. Literally!

A beautiful, red admiral butterfly had fluttered past and overtaken me. Gasping for air, I finally reached the finishing line. Instead of throwing my arms out wide in celebration as I broke the imaginary tape, I leaned against the bonnet of my car, struggling for breath. The adrenaline surge disappeared as quickly as it had arrived. It looked like my forty years of trying to escape from the inevitability of old age was ending. Finally, I had to admit that this was a race I could not win. As I watched, the butterfly lazily completed a lap of honour before setting off, probably to break another old runner's heart. As he disappeared, I began to think back through the decades to where and how my love-hate relationship with running had started.

The mists of memory slowly began to clear as an eleven-year-old version of myself emerged to remind me that butterflies had not always held the upper hand.

Chapter 1

1969: The Summer of Love and a Knife

Running and I had never been natural bedfellows. Some of my earliest school day memories involved the misery and dread I felt at the mere mention of three words, cross-country running.

These fearful words were usually barked out at the class on the wettest and coldest days of the year. I was eleven years old, slightly overweight, and shy. I found myself at a small private school where my elder brother had begun the previous year. The teachers were ferocious, most having served in the Second World War. They frightened the hell out of me, and I could see why Hitler had lost the war. The whole educational system there was run along strict military lines. Orders were shouted, never spoken, and God helped any poor young boy who did not immediately jump when told to do so. We were never allowed to speak unless spoken to. If there were siblings in the school, the eldest was Major and the youngest Minor. I was, therefore, always addressed as Eades Minor. Talk about giving a child an early inferiority complex. Every day, I was constantly reminded that I was second best. I was the Minor to my brother's Major. My only consolation was when three brothers joined, and the youngest consequently was addressed as Minimus. That poor, poor child must have little chance of success in life.

This was my first introduction to running. Never before had anyone insisted that I run for running's sake. We would be herded into a rickety old van, our faces reflecting the terror of what lay ahead. Ten of us would sit on the slatted wooden benches along each side of the barren interior. There was no heater in this old Bedford van, and by the time we reached the foothills of the South Downs, we would all be shivering, and our teeth chattered as we struggled to stay warm. We were then tipped out of the rear doors and told to run up the steep hill. To make it even more unpleasant, if that were possible, the last boy to make it to the top would have to run back down the hill whilst the others were driven back to the start point.

This brutal treatment of young boys would never be allowed to happen today, and it instilled a deep hatred of anything to do with running in my young psyche. If those teachers had intended to scare me away from running, then they certainly succeeded.

As the ten of us set off, I was at the back of the pack. I was not athletic, and my puppy fat was still firmly in place as I puffed and panted my way up the hill. The rest of the class were now tiny figures in the distance, and I knew that I was going to be ridiculed when I finally reached the top and had to do it all again.

And then I heard a small voice behind me. I had forgotten about the only boy in the class who was slower and chubbier than me. A little boy called Blick.

His small, plaintive voice begged me to slow down and wait for him. He feared most things in life, especially getting lost on a cold, wet hill. I stopped and waited for him to catch up with me. We then plodded together up that muddy, frozen, track. Blick was in tears; he knew he would lose and have to do it again in front of his mocking classmates.

As we finally made it to the finish line, I was about to move ahead and leave him to his fate when I had a sudden and unexpected rush of compassion. Instead of overtaking him, I slowed and allowed him to finish ahead of me. I came in last and had to run down the hill. I may have lost the race, but I had made a new best friend, one that I was not sure I really wanted.

Blick was a very odd little boy who always carried a sharp, lethal-looking penknife. He would sit alone in the playground, sharpening this weapon with a blank expression on his face. He rarely spoke to anyone, and unsurprisingly few people would approach a small boy possessing a lethal weapon. Should anyone upset or annoy Blick, he would increase the ferocity of his sharpening. Back and forth, the blade would go against the black flint bar. Tiny sparks would fly everywhere when Blick was troubled or stressed. These days, a van full of police officers in full riot gear would surround and either taser or shoot Blick. This, however, was the late 1960s and Blick's antics were largely ignored by everyone. Indeed, I imagined that most teachers secretly encouraged this type of behaviour. It took them back to their glory days in the war.

Apart from me, Blick had no friends. He was a loner; his knife was his primary companion. After our run, I replaced the knife in Blick's affections, and he followed me around like an abandoned puppy. Everywhere I went, Blick followed. Wherever I sat, he sat next to me. I was beginning to regret my decision to allow Blick to overtake me.

One morning, I was enjoying double Latin. I say enjoying, I meant that I was enduring a lesson totally beyond my comprehension. I always tried to sit at the back of the classroom to avoid any unpleasant questions from Mr Robinson, our Latin teacher. Hiding at the back with me was, of course, Blick. He preferred to be as far away from the teacher as possible to perfect his blade honing. As I struggled with my Latin verbs, my partner was busily sharpening his knife under his desk.

Then as if in slow motion, I saw Blick make a near-fatal mistake. Stroking his knife a little too vigorously, Blick's hand slipped, and the knife went from the flint block onto the inside of his thigh. Slowly, the inside leg of his trousers split apart to reveal a little pudgy white leg. Blick was not an outdoor sort of chap; he preferred to skulk around in dark corners. This was probably the first time his leg had seen daylight since our run. As we both stared in fascination, this little leg followed the same pattern as the trousers had; it opened up from the top of his thigh to just above his knee. Any future Mrs Blick would be very fortunate to find that the blade missed a particular part of Blick's anatomy, although not by much.

At first, nothing seemed to happen. And then, his leg opened up just like a banana being peeled. Blick looked at his leg and then at me with a puzzled expression. He was in no pain and didn't seem particularly worried or upset, just confused. On the other hand, even I knew that this was not good. This diagnosis was further enforced when Blick's femoral artery decided to show just what it could do. The first spurt of blood was just a taster of what was to come.

When you are eleven years old, and in a Latin lesson, you are desperate not to bring attention to yourself. This is especially true if you have a lethal weapon in your possession and are perfectly aware of the consequences of interrupting Mr Robinson's Latin lesson. And so, Blick took the only course of action he thought appropriate. He grabbed his pink school blazer; we really did have to wear a pink blazer. This revolting garment made the walk past the local comprehensive school very challenging as taunts and objects were thrown at us. As Blick pushed his blazer deeper into his crotch, the colour quickly changed from pink to red. At least his walk past the comprehensive school would now be safer.

I knew Blick's answer to his problem was a very short-term solution. There was, by now, very little of the pink blazer showing. Instead, it was an even deeper red. On the other hand, the source of all this blood was now beginning to look very pale. Something had to be done and be done quickly. Summoning up all my courage, I put my hand up, not something I liked doing in a Latin class.

Immediately, Mr Robinson shouted at me to put my hand down. He had not asked any questions that needed answering. I stuttered the word "Sir" and was again shouted at to be quiet. I stood up and desperately repeated the phrase. Mr Robinson was not a man to be disobeyed. His face went a strange purple-ish colour as he shouted at me to get out of his class and report to the headmaster's study, a familiar journey that sadly, I knew well. Standing my ground, I pleaded with my schoolmaster to listen to me. The classroom went deathly quiet. Nobody, literally nobody, ever answered back to Mr Robinson. The room was long and narrow; Mr Robinson stood at one end and I at the other, like a couple of cowboys in a tableau of a gunfight waiting to draw their guns. Finally, 1 broke away from his stare to look at Blick, who by this time, had laid his head on his desk; he appeared lifeless.

My head snapped back to look again at the fearsome Mr Robinson as he shouted at me to get out of his classroom.

"I think Blick is dead, Sir," seemed to take the wind out of Mr Robinson's sails, at least for a while.

"Don't be stupid, boy. Just get out," came the reply.

"But sir."

"Get out."

"No, Sir."

Mr Robinson was in the latter stages of his life. He had not been blessed with good looks or an athletic physique. Yet this rotund little man covered the distance between us at a remarkable speed. Simultaneously, he also managed to get his ever-present cane well above his head, 'a fine achievement', I thought to myself.

As the cane descended towards my shoulder, Mr Robinson became aware of a vast, dark patch of liquid pooled beneath Blick's desk. By another feat of unexpected agility, he avoided slipping into this puddle. Stopping next to the now apparently lifeless form that used to be Blick, Mr Robinson stared transfixed at the scene in front of him. His mouth fell wide open as he tried to comprehend the gruesome scene.

Shouting at the class to leave the room, Mr Robinson went into overdrive. Snatching the blazer away, he asked me what had happened. Apparently, schoolboys do generally not come apart at the seams for no reason. I quickly explained what I had seen and how the injury had occurred.

Decades later, I remember how the fearsome teacher instantly changed from an ogre to a hero. Within moments, he had applied pressure on the ruptured artery and had stemmed the flow of blood. In a quiet, authoritative, but kindly voice, he asked me to find the school nurse and ask her to call an ambulance. Later, I learned that Mr Robinson was a decorated war hero, and unlike a number of his colleagues, he had chosen not to use his military title in civilian life. Mr Robinson had obviously attended the wounded before; he literally saved that young boy's life.

Twenty minutes later, Blick had been deposited at the local hospital, and a very apologetic Mr Robinson had become a friend. Finally, as I left the classroom, after answering the headmaster's questions, I noticed a shiny object under my desk. Retrieving the penknife and giving it a quick clean, I put it in my pocket for when its owner returned.

Blick was never to return to that school. Apparently, he had other problems more pressing than a severed artery. He was sent to an institution which dealt with such things.

On the upside, I had inherited a very sharp knife. I kept this memento for many years, sadly losing it on a camping trip. It was a loss, although not a significant loss. By that time I lost it, the knife was totally blunt; I had learnt a valuable lesson about trying to sharpen knives.

Blick was now gone. My main focus now was getting out of the dreaded cross-country run. With the only runner slower than myself now being put back together again, I was doomed to a series of last places and subsequent punishments.

To put it mildly, I was not too fond of running. Literally, I hated every wet, cold, and miserable step. I vowed to myself that when I could make my own decisions, I would never, ever put on a pair of running shoes again.

This book is about how my older self let that poor, wet, cold, sad and vulnerable little boy down. To my younger self, I am genuinely very sorry. To everyone else, this is the story of how a non-runner, in the truest sense, ran the world. Well, the bits that I visited anyway.

Chapter 2

New Trousers

Throughout the remainder of my education, I remained a strict non-runner. Although I loved sport, running for the sake of running remained well and truly off my list of things to do. I enjoyed rugby and played for the first team throughout my time at the local grammar school. However, I only ever ran if I actually had to run. The coach would shout at me during training sessions as I stood around whilst everyone else sprinted up and down the pitch. Instead of running, I would practise my kicking and ball-handling skills. After the warm-up, I was happy to run up and down the pitch, passing and kicking the ball. This, to me, was not running simply for the sake of running. It was running with a purpose. I was happy to sprint after the ball or the player with the ball. I would run for the whole of the training session, just as long as I didn't have to run for no reason other than running for running's sake.

I loved cricket, and as a fast bowler with a very long run-up, I would cover many kilometres over a match as I tore in at full pace to deliver the ball as quickly as possible. I played tennis for hours, making up for my lack of skill with an ability to get to almost any ball that came my way. I was very happy with a life which did not involve or necessitate just running. During the short time that I attended university, I followed the same pattern with lots of rugby and absolutely no running. Then, one day, everything changed. The time that I had to earn a living had arrived.

My chosen career was to become an airline pilot. As I was quick to find out, rugby and flying do not go together terribly well. Having fifteen large, usually very ugly, players trying to knock the hell out of you on weekends is not conducive to a long and happy flying career. Very strict medical regulations clearly state that a pilot requires both eyes, ears, arms and legs and being incapacitated through team sports is not an acceptable exemption. Conversely, very strict rugby rules require you to remove or attempt to remove at least one of these appendages from an opposition player. One of these activities had to go. As there was no way I could earn a living as a very ordinary rugby player, I decided to concentrate on becoming a very ordinary pilot. From that moment on, all my sporting activity ceased, and I became adept at being the ultimate couch potato. To be fair, I had little or no time for any leisure activity and trying to learn to fly took all my time and energy.

Initially, I managed to keep fit by loading luggage onto aircraft, enabling me to pay for my flying lessons. This involved heavy manual work, and I managed to keep fit and maintain my ideal weight without really having to think about it. As my flying career advanced, I spent more time in the cockpit and less time heaving bags around. As I progressed from learning to fly to teaching people to fly, I found most of my physical activity had ceased. Instead, I would arrive at the flying school each morning and sit in the clubhouse, drinking coffee and eating endless chocolate bars. Occasionally, when the weather permitted, I would fly around the south coast of England, teaching my pupils to fly. After a few months of indulging in this very sedentary lifestyle, I began to notice that my trousers were shrinking. The same thing was happening to my belt and shirt. I vowed to buy better quality clothing that did not shrink after a couple of washes.

Still refusing to consider any other explanation for my poorly fitting and tight attire, I continued to eat and fly. Kit Kats were supplemented with wonderfully delicious Wagon Wheels. These large, round chocolate biscuit treats, popular in the seventies, were filled with jam, marshmallows and about a thousand calories. My taste buds were incredibly happy, but my trousers continued to get smaller. And then, the inevitable happened: I found out that, in reality, I was actually overweight.

The truth dawned on me during a training flight in a tiny two-seater aircraft on a hot, sunny day. My student was doing a grand job of trying to make me airsick. He managed to get the aircraft into positions that I had never seen before as we attempted to spin our aircraft earthwards. Each time we corrected one mistake, he would find another to amaze me. My seatbelt was uncomfortably tight, and after completing our aerobatics, I thought I would loosen it a little bit for the flight home. Reaching down, I attempted to adjust the belt. Pull and push as much as I could, the belt remained unpleasantly tight. As I struggled to loosen the belt, I noticed something strange and unfamiliar above my waistline. Grabbing hold and squeezing just to make sure, my blood ran cold at the realisation that what I was holding was actually part of me that had never previously been there. In a matter of months, I had gone from a strapping youth to a man with a robust middle-aged spread. The remainder of the flight was spent cursing the Kit Kats, and I even reserved a bit of anger for my favourite chocolate biscuit, the dreaded Wagon Wheel.

Trudging back to the clubhouse, I quickly debriefed my student; I think I advised him to try sailing instead, anything that did not involve his recklessly uncontrolled spinning through the air. I went to the toilet to check that my mind was not deceiving me. I undid my shirt and looked into the full-length mirror.

I was shocked at the reflection that stared back at me. Was this really me? Pushing above my belt was a plentiful and unmistakable roll of chocolate bars and beer. My clothes did not seem to fit me anymore. How the hell had I not noticed this until now? Either that or I had put on the wrong trousers this morning.

Things had to change and change quickly. I considered quitting beer, but that was too drastic. Instead, the chocolate had to go. I also made a promise to myself that I kept for the next forty years. To fix this, I would take up running. I felt terribly guilty that I would have to go against everything my eleven-year-old self had endured through this tortuous sport, but there was no alternative. Running was the only form of exercise that I could do anywhere and could do alone and at no cost. Team sports were out as I was rarely around at weekends. Other sports took up too much time, a very rare commodity in those early flying days. No, it had to be running or buying a new and larger pair of new trousers.

Chapter 3

Where to Start

Driving home later that day, I felt a certain amount of relief. I had identified and accepted my weight problem. Like an alcoholic admitting their excessive drinking, it was the first step on the road to recovery, or so I thought.

Full of my newfound enthusiasm for running, I went in search of the appropriate attire for my first run. At the time, I was living in a very small flat in Worthing on the Sussex coast. As I only had one small chest of drawers, it didn't take long to discover that I only had one pair of ancient and tattered shorts. Holding up this rather dubious article of clothing at a respectable distance, I examined the shorts in more detail. I now realised why my socks and underpants always had a somewhat musty smell. The shorts still bore the residue of my last rugby match over a year ago. Dried mud clung to the material in a bizarre pattern. As I held the shorts up to the light, I could also make out the grass stains down one side, obviously the result of a brave sliding tackle. For a moment, a flood of sporting memories poured over me. I was tempted to re-join my local rugby club and forget the ridiculous idea of running for running's sake. What on earth had I been thinking? Of course, the answer to my problem was more rugby. This new idea lasted as long as it took me to discover the mouth guard in the shorts pocket. As I pulled this rubber appendage out to examine it, I could still see the dried blood clinging to the inside of the guard. Memories of being punched squarely on the jaw as I attempted to retrieve the ball from the back of the scrum flooded back. Walking into the kitchen, I dropped the mouthguard in the bin and the shorts into the sink. Rugby was in my past. The future lay in the sink. As my shorts slowly sank to soak to the bottom of the washing bowl, I looked at my reflection in the water. 'My God, is that the start of a double chin?' I thought to myself in horror. Slowly, the water was turning dark brown, thankfully hiding this apparition. The time had definitely arrived to find a running top and a pair of trainers. I was nearly ready to start my new adventure.

The next morning, my alarm woke me a full hour before my regular, pretty relaxed routine for starting my day usually began. Rolling over, my hand slammed down on the clock as I attempted to silence the ringing in my ears. I flopped over and went back to sleep. This running lark could wait another day. I needed my rest. Sadly, my alarm clock was subsequently disabled, and I found myself rushing late to the airport for my first flight of the day. My student gave me a sympathetic look as I explained the reason for my late arrival. As we taxied the little aircraft across the grass airfield at Shoreham Airport, I attempted again to make myself comfortable in the seat. I would have to reduce my size or find a bigger aircraft. I had to find another way to fit this running lark into my life. Getting up ridiculously early was obviously not going to work for me.

Over the next few weeks, I did my best to run at least once a week. I absolutely hated and dreaded every single step of every single run. It took me hours to work up the enthusiasm to set off on another thirty minutes of sheer torture. Just putting on my running gear was an effort. I would start with my running top. I would put it on and then go about whatever I was doing. Thirty minutes later, I would change into my running shorts. By this time in the proceedings, I had managed to dispose of the ancient, stained rugby shorts and had bought a pair of 'go faster' running shorts. Unfortunately, I purchased these without taking any help or advice. They were far too small, barely covering the all-important bits that would get me arrested if I exposed them to an unsuspecting public. I looked ridiculous, and it only took a few stares and laughs before these new shorts followed their predecessors into the rubbish bin. Once correctly attired, I would then walk around in my tiny flat until I worked up the enthusiasm needed to put my socks on.

Finally, I would approach my newly purchased running shoes. I soon discovered that wet running shoes quickly developed the sort of odour that could have served as a gaseous weapon of war. Throw a couple of these size twelve shoes into the German trenches in the First World War, and the surrender would have been hastened. These offensive articles now lived permanently on the pavement at the entrance to my flat. At first, I was worried that any passer-by could steal my new purchases. Not surprisingly, very few people passed after I started leaving my shoes outside. Once I had worked up the courage to bring in and put my shoes on, there was no going back. Only forward motion could protect me from the odour. Fully attired, I now had no choice but to run. The thought of taking everything off and going back inside would be a humiliation and failure that was beyond imagination.

Those first few tentative runs almost put me off for life. I made a curious figure in my micro shorts as I jogged, not ran, through the local streets. I felt very self-conscious and extremely uncomfortable as I puffed and panted my way along the busy roads. In those early days of the 1980s, running was something you did to get away from the local police, not something you did for pleasure. I noticed people staring at me, especially as my micro shorts had started disappearing into my bottom. I must have looked like the local pervert up to no good, someone who needed to be put behind bars as soon as possible. I had learned two fundamental lessons the hard way. Buy a proper pair of comfortable shorts and choose quieter, less populated streets to run along. These early runs should and could have put me off the sport for life. However, I was beginning to feel a little less like a baby elephant at the end of each run. With the proper attire and clean, almost odour-free shoes, I was finally beginning to reap some of the benefits of exercise. My trousers were slightly more comfortable, and my shirts began to feel slightly looser. Maybe, just maybe, there might be something to this running game after all. I would be fine without a larger aircraft if I continued like this. This was just as well, as the flying school I worked for didn't have any bigger planes.

Chapter 4

Finding the Time

The next few years were incredibly hectic. I was working full time, trying to gain my commercial flying licence. The days were spent teaching students to fly. The evenings were dedicated to self-study in order to pass the numerous technical examinations that lay ahead. As well as my flying instructor's job, I had to earn extra money to pay for my upcoming ground and flying examinations. This left very little time to pursue my new running regime. I did my best to keep my weight in check. I tried to be careful with what I ate and tried not to succumb to the ever-present temptation of mid-morning, late morning, early afternoon and late afternoon snacks. I was often unsuccessful in those quests. I started running in between flying lessons. There was the occasional time when I had a spare hour between students. I would set off from the flying club and run along the perimeter road, puffing as I went and trying to keep one eye out for potholes and the other one for our club aircraft as they flew around the aerodrome. I managed to get some very close views of some very good, and some very bad, landings. I just hoped that the good ones were my students. The downside to this was that whilst I stared into the sky, I fell over a lot. The track was in very poor condition, and you needed to have your wits about you if you were to avoid the numerous potholes. Running and staring at the sky eventually produced one fall too many. Injured and pained, I returned, like an addict, to eating the Kit Kats and Wagon Wheels between lessons. The downside was that, of course, the aircraft seatbelts began to get tighter again. The upside was that the poor students were not subjected to a hot, sweaty instructor moaning about how much his last fall had hurt.

For the next few years, running and I became distant companions. We would write to each other occasionally and send each other Christmas cards. Apart from that, we were effectively estranged. I did manage to curtail my addiction to all things sweet, and therefore, I could still fit into the tiny training aircraft that were my offices in the sky. I would occasionally admit to myself that I was secretly quite pleased that I did not have to subject myself to the rigours of running. My eleven-year-old self and I had relaxed into a physically sedate lifestyle once more.

Eventually, the commercial flying exams came and went and I found myself the proud owner of a shiny new commercial pilot's licence. I was finally released from the restrictions of being a flying instructor and could literally spread my wings and join the airlines. Sadly, none of them wanted me. I went into business aviation instead.

As I struggled to find my way up the aviation ladder, I managed to start flying larger aircraft on commercial routes. This started with small propeller aircraft and progressed to business jets. I now had little or no excuse not to rekindle my affair with running. I no longer spent my days and nights teaching and studying. I would now fly somewhere and stay for a number of hours or return the next day.

This meant that I now had time on my hands, time that could be spent running and not devouring the food and champagne left behind by my very wealthy passengers. The need for more physical exercise in my life was brought sharply into focus on one memorable trip. My best friend, Peter Brown and I, had flown a number of executives to Deelan in the Netherlands. We were due to fly back to London the following morning. As we always did, after the passengers had disembarked, we cleaned and prepared the aircraft for the return flight before we set off for the hotel. On this particular trip, we had loaded catering for eight, hopefully hungry passengers. In fact, what we had were eight people who had already eaten and were not interested in all the treats we had provided. Consequently, we were left with eight untouched servings of the most delicious food. There were plates full of temptations, which would all have to go to waste if we did not do the decent thing and take our prize back to the hotel with us.

The hotel staff gave us some very strange looks as we walked, well struggled, into the reception area carrying plates of food. The two of us stood there in our pilot's uniforms, looking for all the world like overdressed caterers, not professional pilots. Making a lame joke about the quality of the food served in the hotel, we took our hoard into one of our rooms to be devoured at our leisure.

Two hours later, eight full servings had been consumed by two people. It was only comparable to the feeling you get after a particularly good Christmas lunch when all you wanted to do was lie down on the settee and go to sleep. It was only early afternoon, and our guilt at our gluttony persuaded us to make use of the hotel's tennis court rather than idle the afternoon away. Twenty minutes later, it was obvious that sheer gluttony followed by exercise does not go together terribly well. We returned to our rooms clutching aching stomachs, vowing never to be so greedy again. For my part, I knew that I had no choice but to write a begging letter to my old friend, running. We really had to get back together again.

This period of my flying career involved flying an executive jet around the United Kingdom and Europe. Most flights left early in the morning, and we often landed late at night. Companies would charter our aircraft to avoid their highly paid executives staying away for a moment longer than necessary. We took off before the short haul commercial airline pilots had woken up and landed when they were safely tucked up in bed. The flying was great fun but left very little time to put on my running shoes and hit the pavement. I tried running whilst we awaited the return of our passengers. There were two main drawbacks. Firstly, we had to be ready to fly at a moment's notice if their plans changed, and secondly, none of these dynamic business types wanted to be greeted and flown home by a hot, sweaty, dishevelled pilot. Once again, running and I became distant friends. Of course, I would set out on the occasional run on my days off. This was way before anybody had heard of a mobile, let alone a smartphone. My partner, Pete, and I had set up our own little executive jet operation. We were the only two full-time employees. In the early days, we had to be ready to fly at a moment's notice. The office telephone would ring, and within the hour, we would be racing down the runway at Gatwick. We flew spares for ships all over Europe. We had our aircraft adapted into an air ambulance. Insurance companies would lease the aircraft to repatriate stricken clients from foreign hospitals. Therefore, I could hardly set off on a run and leave an empty office or aircraft. In those heady days of our new business, we rarely had any time to ourselves.

The weeks and months would glide by without me so much as looking at a running shoe, never mind putting one on. My running gear would lie untouched for months, and the occasional time I managed to set off, I was usually too exhausted to finish the run. Executive aviation and running did not mix at all well. I was heading towards middle age and another middle-aged spread. Luckily for me and my waistline, a new beginning was just around the corner.

Chapter 5

Let the Running Begin, Well Almost!

In 1987, I changed from executive aviation, into the big bad world of the commercial airlines. I left behind the small executive aircraft that had been my career for the past seven years. I now started to fly the wonderful Boeing 747 and began a love affair with this aircraft that would last for the next thirty-four years.

Apart from the obvious change to my professional career, I now had time on my hands, with nothing stopping me from running. I was flying long-haul routes, and the 747 took me all over the world. There were no 'there and back' return day flights now. A trip now meant a minimum of three days and up to two weeks away from home. Once we had checked into a hotel, our time was our own until we were picked up for the next flight. A typical three-day trip would involve a seven-hour flight to the east coast of America or Canada. We would then have twenty-four hours in a city before flying home. This usually meant a daylight flight out followed by a night flight home. This gave me a whole day to think of a reason not to run. Luckily for my health, I usually failed to think of any valid excuse to sit in my room. I started to run in New York, Boston, Toronto, and Montreal. I would run in conditions as varied as the great ice storm of Montreal to the crushingly hot summer days of Miami, sometimes within the same week.

I was a very junior pilot at British Airways in the late 1980s. I rarely got to fly to more popular destinations such as South Africa, Australia or the Caribbean. However, I was happy with my lot. For the first time, finally, I decided to give running the attention and commitment it deserved. And then Liz and I decided to get married and start a family.

Having children is the most rewarding and exciting thing I have ever done. A new baby changes everything. It puts everything in your life into perspective. You are no longer the centre of your own universe. There are so many positives to being a parent. The one thing that parenting does not give you is enough time to sleep. I now found myself flying six, sometimes seven, trips across the Atlantic every month. I was also trying to provide Liz, my long-suffering wife, some respite and rest when I returned home. We were both exhausted for most of the time. No longer would I arrive in New York and plan a run the next day before flying home. Now I would plan to sleep, and I got very good at it, very quickly. On one memorable occasion, we arrived in Boston at lunchtime. The crew planned to meet at six that evening for a well-deserved beer. I set my alarm clock for five and tried to catch a few hours' sleep. I must have sleepily silenced the alarm when it bleeped, as the next thing I knew, the telephone was ringing. Picking it up and about to apologise for being late for a beer. I was astounded to hear the pre-recorded message telling me that my pick-up for the flight home was in an hour. It took me a few moments to realise that I had literally slept for twenty-four hours. Not only that, but I had laid down on the bed in my uniform and had fallen into a deep sleep, fully dressed. I had a hectic hour trying to iron my uniform trousers and jacket. I looked more like a homeless person than an airline pilot.

Another memorable parenting moment was when I returned home from an overnight flight. Poor Liz had had a terrible time whilst I was away, looking after a baby who stubbornly refused to sleep. Two nights of being awake and trying to comfort a child who was starting to teethe had left her totally exhausted. As I climbed into bed, I was grateful that I only had to fly an aircraft. After a few hours of blissful sleep, I awoke feeling refreshed and ready for a run.

Instead, I found myself sitting up in bed, looking down at this beautiful child who had been placed in my arms. James had now quietened down and was slowly falling asleep. He seemed so relaxed and angelic I was beginning to doubt my wife's story of sleepless nights.

The next thing I knew, a screaming baby was lying on the floor. I had committed the terrible sin of falling back to sleep whilst trying to soothe the baby. Not only had I fallen asleep, but I had also dropped the baby onto the floor. Jumping out of bed, I scooped James up and did my best to calm him down. He was used to being cuddled when he cried, not being thrown away like an unwanted toy. Of course, his mother instantly knew the difference between a cry of teething pains and the "my father had just dropped me" cry. The bedroom door flew open, the baby was snatched from my grasp, and the door again slammed shut.

I lay there for a moment, not quite sure what to do. Did I try to apologise? Did I offer to have another go at getting James to sleep? I was still unsure of the best course of action as Liz took the baby away to somewhere safe. Being a father, a long-haul pilot, and a runner was proving more difficult than I thought.

Rightly, running took a back seat as I tried my best to juggle flying and parenthood for the next year. I did manage a few half-hearted runs down route. However, sleep was such a scarce commodity that it always took priority over everything else. Eventually, and blessedly, James began to settle down to a regular routine. He decided that nights were for sleeping, not screaming, and his parents were finally able to return to a semblance of normality. Once again, I started to pack my running shoes when I left home on another trip.

Five years later we were blessed with another son, Robert. Either we had learnt from our previous mistakes or Rob was just as keen on a full night's sleep as we were. I was able to sleep and run with our new baby in the house.

Circumstances had changed at work. I had managed to transfer from Heathrow to Gatwick. This meant that the routes I flew were very different. Gatwick flights were mainly for leisure, not business. Instead of the East Coast of America, I primarily flew to the Caribbean, still on the Boeing 747 Jumbo Jet. My trips were now an average of five days, not the three days I was used to. Instead of twenty-four hours, I now had two or three days off down route. It was time to dust off those running shoes. My running adventures were about to begin in earnest, and so began my newly discovered and enduring passion, becoming someone who ran for the sheer joy of running.

Chapter 6

Live and Let Live

With my running gear safely packed away in my suitcase, I set off for a flight to Montego Bay, Jamaica. This was not my first visit to this beautiful Island. I had been lucky enough to visit on a couple of previous occasions. The approach was spectacular as we descended over the azure-blue Caribbean Sea. I could not help but notice the miles of golden, sandy beaches awaiting our arrival. There were no let down or approach aids to guide us onto the short runway. The entire approach was flown visually, which always made for an exciting and ultimately rewarding approach and landing.

As we boarded the crew bus for the relatively short drive to the hotel, I felt rather pleased with myself; it had been a good flight. Twenty-two of us were on the bus, a rickety old contraption that would spectacularly fail any MOT test at home.

There was no room for the twenty-two suitcases that luckily, had followed us from London. Instead, the crew luggage had been loaded separately into an equally antiquated van. With the baggage van leading the way, our small convoy coughed and sputtered its way onto the narrow, pockmarked road that eventually, would take us to the hotel.

All went well for the first few minutes. Some of the crew had brought along refreshments from the aircraft. These were very alcoholic beverages, which were being consumed at an alarming rate after a long flight.

I was sitting at the front of the bus. As I intended to go for a run when we reached the hotel, I refused any drinks politely, no matter how insistent the offer was. Anyway, it would make my first beer after a long run even more welcome. I watched the baggage bus as it bellowed out vast plumes of black smoke as we began the climb up a steep hill. And then, an unthinkable, but somehow, unsurprising thing happened. Twenty-two heavy suitcases, which had been thrown into the bus, slid inexorably towards the rear doors. Like the rest of the bus, these doors had seen much better days. Instead of metal latches, these doors were tied closed with an old rope. Unfortunately, whoever had tied these ropes together was more skilled at tying slip knots than tying a knot that would hold the doors closed. Suddenly, the knot gave way, and the two doors flew open under the pressure of the suitcases piled against them. One by one, the cases exited the back of the bus at some speed. As they hit the tarmac, they exploded like little mini land mines. Each suitcase followed a similar pattern to the one before. The case would slide out of the back of the bag bus and turn over in mid-air. As the case struck the road, it would fly open and disgorge its contents over the other road users. Shirts, shoes, dresses, blouses, and swimwear passed over and around our bus. Our driver was busy swerving to avoid each case as it landed directly in front of us. The crew, drinks in hand, were being violently thrown from side to side. There were, of course, no seatbelts on the bus. Within moments, the entire crew were wearing their drinks. The majority of these drinks were known as 'Brown Milk'. This was a dangerous mixture of any spirits leftover from the flight combined with milk. The milk was meant to disguise the cocktails' true nature from prying eyes. They were very potent, and if they were emptied onto, instead of into, a person, they had basically the same effect; you very quickly looked and felt dreadful.

By this time, both buses had reached the top of the hill. The flat road meant the cases still fell out, but at a slower rate. When the lorry hit a not infrequent bump or pothole, the bags again flew out at an alarming rate. Our driver was honking and flashing at the other driver in an attempt to stop him. Sadly, he was probably playing Bob Marley at full volume and enjoying the sea views. He was far too preoccupied to look in his mirror to see what was happening behind him. Our bus was in complete chaos. The crew screamed as they wiped the brown milk from their eyes, only to see their underwear fly past the bus windows. The occasional suitcase would strike the bus with the sound of a thunderclap and then, it would disintegrate entirely. There were screams to stop the bus and other cries to overtake the bag bus and stop it from disgorging any more bags. Our driver decided to literally take the middle road and line of least resistance and followed the bag bus for the last mile to the hotel.

Both buses spluttered to a halt outside the imposing entrance to our five-star hotel, which had previously served as a colonial mansion. Two smartly uniformed stewards stood by two white columns supporting the entrance canopy. Equally smartly dressed guests milled around, enjoying the views and tranquillity. It was all very 'Great Gatsby' until twenty-two British Airways crew members staggered out of the bus covered in a white layer of sticky brown milk. The majority were still screaming or crying. The bus drivers joined in the general melee and began shouting and screaming at each other, adding to the commotion. I had always thought that Rastas believed in peace and love. That illusion was shattered after the first punch was thrown.

Amid all this excitement, only one person had managed to avoid the brown milk fate. The one person who had refused a drink, the only person who was, in fact, planning on still going for a run. In my pristine uniform, I wandered to the bag bus, leaving the rest of my crew dripping brown liquid all over the hotel's red carpet. I reached into one of the doors and peered inside. Where there had previously been twenty-two suitcases, there now remained only one. As all crews usually brought a Delsey suitcase, it was often impossible to tell which was yours until you checked the yellow crew label. With very little hope, I clambered into the bus and pulled the solitary bag towards me. Unbelievably, there was the yellow crew label with my name on it. Not only had I avoided being covered in a sticky brown mess, but I was also the only crew member whose luggage had survived intact.

Sheepishly, I carried the case from the bus and attempted to sneak past the still-traumatised crew. It was late afternoon, and I wanted to get my run in before it got dark. There was little I could do to help my colleagues, and rather than just stand there, I thought that the fewer people blocking the hotel's entrance, the better. With a few expletives ringing in my ears, I shuffled off to find my room. I consoled myself with the thought that I was about to do something productive, and I was sure that the crew would understand, eventually. Had I been more considerate and empathetic, I would have avoided being held at knifepoint an hour later. Now, who would have the last laugh? If my suitcase had joined its fellows and spread all its contents on the road, I would not have had any running gear and sensibly would have gone to the terrace bar as had the rest of the crew.

Instead, I found myself running back along the road we had just driven along. Our bus drivers were retracing their steps and attempting to retrieve any remaining articles of clothing. Their main problem was that the locals had suddenly discovered this windfall of gifts and rightly or wrongly, decided that 'finders keepers' was the order of the day. I could see little reason to join in the many tug-of-war competitions being played out in the middle of the road. Traffic was at a standstill, and I noticed that quite a few of the cars had been abandoned as their drivers joined in the treasure hunt.

Our hotel was part of the Rose Hall estate. This was the famous estate of the White Witch of Montego Bay, Annie Palmer. Legend had it that in the 1800s, this evil plantation owner had murdered her three husbands and numerous enslaved people. She ruled through the use of voodoo and extreme violence. She was rewarded with a golf course named after her. I decided to head to this course and the ghost of Annie Palmer. This had the advantage of avoiding the crowds of onlookers and bounty hunters on the road. There would be many people wearing British Airways uniforms in town that night.

As I left the chaos behind me, I noticed a track that led directly onto the golf course. It looked very inviting after the mess behind me. The golf course was stunning, my favourite type, with long, wide fairways, most with a view of the ocean. It was starting to get a little late; the sun was fast making its way down onto the horizon. As is typical in the Caribbean, there is little time for dusk. One moment, the sun is there in all its glory, and before you realise it, the sun disappears with one final flourish of a stunning sunset. Montego Bay in the late 1980s was not the sort of place you would want to be alone after dark in such a remote setting.

At this time, large corporations were rapidly discovering this paradise's potential and were building vast hotel complexes. They would also buy the shoreline alongside these hotels for the exclusive use of their guests. To top it all, they made these eyesores all-inclusive. They flew in the majority of their food and drink directly from the United States. This left the local population angered and bewildered. Beaches that had been their playgrounds for generations were now being denied to them. They saw crowds of tourists arriving and then ferried into these all-inclusive monstrosities. The tourists only came out of their compounds for conducted tours and rarely, if ever, ventured out to spend their money in the local community. Nearby restaurants, which had previously relied on the tourist trade, found themselves without customers. Many that had been around for generations had to close down whilst lorries carrying pre-packaged and refrigerated food rumbled past to supply the hotel kitchens. This toxic situation created an understandable resentment towards tourists and holiday companies. In this volatile environment, a rather shabby, white male runner strode towards his hotel in the semi-darkness. What could possibly go wrong? I was soon to find out.

For those of a particular vintage who grew up with Roger Moore as James Bond, many will remember a famous scene from the film *Live and Let Die*. Our hero makes yet another conquest, this time, underneath a waterfall set amongst rolling hills. It was at this precise geographical moment that I found myself needing to summon my inner James Bond. I had now been running for nearly an hour. The temperature was still sweltering, and I was very hot and sweaty. I could almost smell and taste my second beer; the first would not even touch the sides. I only had about five minutes left as the golf course was part of our hotel's grounds. I was idly hoping that our crew had recovered some of their possessions when that idle speculation became the least of my worries.

As I passed a clump of tall bushes and vegetation at the side of the waterfall, two spectres appeared directly in front of me. Immediately, I knew that I was in trouble. My instinct was to try to outrun them. However, they were younger and looked a lot fitter than me. Also, they had not just flown an aeroplane for the past ten hours and then run solidly for the last hour. So instead of running, I stopped and inquired if I could assist them.

I was using, or trying to use, my best and most friendly demeanour. It didn't seem to be working.

They began to demand money, and a lot of it. Politely, I tried to explain that I had only just landed in their wonderful country and had not had the opportunity to acquire any funds. This did not go down well; their whole attitude instantly became more threatening. To my horror, I noticed that they were both carrying knives. Although I had not yet been directly threatened with these evil-looking implements, they ensured I was aware of their presence. I turned out my pockets to prove I had no money. I wore no watch or jewellery, a habit I had long been practising for obvious reasons. The only thing I had of value was my running shoes, and I was more than prepared to offer them up in exchange for my safety. I'm not sure that James Bond would have thought of this, but again I had to admit that I had never seen Roger Moore in his running gear. I was about to suggest this compromise when I noticed they were wearing brand-new designer trainers. I pointed this out and, showing them my dirty and worn-out shoes, I suggested that, seemingly, it was myself that was more in need of money.

Humour was a gamble that could have gone very badly wrong. Had it gone differently, I would not be here today to tell the story. Luckily for me, they both saw the amusing and absurd predicament that we were in. They had not stopped a rich tourist carrying vast amounts of money. Apparently, they had mugged someone more in need of cash than them. We began to talk. I asked them if they had seen the chaos on the road a while ago. They admitted that they had and were even lucky enough to have benefitted from some of the lost property. I explained that I was part of the British Airways crew who had so carelessly thrown their possessions all over the road.

Unexpectedly, this seemed to appease and amuse my would-be assailants. They approved of British Airways. Apparently, the majority of our passengers stayed in the traditional hotels and visited local shops and restaurants. They went on to complain about what was happening to their towns and villages. What started as a mugging was turning into a political speech. I had to admit that I had a lot of sympathy for what they described.

It slowly dawned on me that these two young men weren't hardened criminals; they were frustrated, out-of-work teenagers. They could not find work or even enjoy a swim on their local beaches. An idea was slowly forming in my mind. To be honest, most of my ideas formed slowly. My heart rate was returning to normal as I realised I was not in immediate danger. As my thoughts of being subjected to violence reduced, my thoughts of cold beer quickly returned.

One of the great things about airline crews is that they can always find the cheapest way to buy wine and beer. Literally anywhere in the world, they would sniff out the best deals. This was particularly true if the crew was lucky enough to have a flight engineer amongst their number. We had a flight engineer, and luckily, one of the best. True to form, he had discovered that a beer bus would stop outside the hotel every night. They sold beer at a tenth of the price the hotel charged. We would meet the bus, buy a couple of crates and have a room party in one unfortunate crew member's room. This beer bus was due to arrive in an hour.

Asking my would-be assailants if they knew about the bus and where it stopped. They confirmed that they knew of its existence but could not afford the beer. I offered to buy them not one beer but a crate of beers. It was now their turn to be shocked and surprised. Their initial reaction was one of great suspicion and anger. They accused me of taking them for fools. They said I was sure to inform the police, and they would be arrested immediately if they turned up. I assured them that they had done nothing to be charged with. They had simply stopped me to have a chat, which was all they had done.

After a few minutes of deliberation, I informed them that if I got going soon, I would have time to get back, have a quick shower and collect some money for the beer. Shrugging their shoulders and looking at this mad Englishman, they disappeared into the gloom as quickly as they had appeared.

Just over an hour later, I was queuing at the beer bus with other crew members to buy our room party supplies. A few had managed to retrieve some clothing, whilst others had purchased items from the hotel shops. We made an incongruous sight as we queued with the locals. As I reached the front of the queue, two apparitions suddenly appeared at my side. My golf course acquaintances had managed to reappear as if by magic. They were looking from side to side to make sure that there were no police in the vicinity. Reassured, they turned to me, half expecting to be turned away. Instead, I handed them a case of twelve beers, which had cost me roughly the same as one pint of beer at home. Thanking me for keeping my word, they again performed their disappearing act, gone before we realised it.

The flight engineer looked at me with a quizzical look on his face.

"Who the hell were they?" he inquired.

Before I had time to relate my adventure, he asked me why one of them was wearing the shirt he had lost on the way to the hotel. Quickly, I changed the subject and went on to drink one too many beers that evening.

Chapter 7

Sale or Return

Antigua was now one of my favourite Caribbean destinations. This little jewel in the Lesser Antilles is paired with the smaller island of Barbuda to the north. Both islands are lovely, friendly and welcoming. Antigua was also an excellent place for running.

When I first started to fly to Antigua, we stayed in the northeast corner at Deep Bay Beach alongside Five Island Village. I had only been running for a relatively short period, and my fitness levels could have been better. I had not appreciated how different it was to run in the heat of a Caribbean day compared to an English summer's day. And so, in my naivety, I set off for a ten-kilometre run at midday. Initially, I had intended to do an early morning run. However, after a late night and probably one beer too many, the early morning had long since departed when finally, I managed to lace up my running shoes and set off into the glare of a blazing sun. As I left the hotel grounds, I attracted curious glances from people sitting in the shade or swimming in the hotel pool.

'More fool them lazing the day away', I thought as I headed inland towards my first turning point. I planned to run towards Yapton Beach, around a large inland lagoon, and then end my run along Deep Bay Beach. From there, I would finally end up back at my hotel. As with all my runs, I tried to make this one a circular route. I know it is all psychological, but if I run somewhere and have to turn around and run back, then half the time, I'm getting further away from the end of my run. On the way back, I'm constantly thinking, 'I've been here before'. No, it's much better to find a circular route. Then, every step forward is also a step closer to finishing. And so, with my route planned, I ran into an ever-hotter day without giving the slightest thought to hydration or sunburn. No, I was a man on a mission. No hangover, common sense, or any appreciation of the conditions would get in my way. 'I was Mr Invincible', or so I thought. There have been three other times whilst running that extreme heat has negatively affected my health. This was the first of them, the other two come later in the book.

I was still naive enough to think that heat exhaustion was something I could run through. Instead of stopping in the shade, I pushed on, but not for long. Luckily for me, the last part of the run was along a sandy beach. By the time I reached the shore, I had accepted that I needed to cool down. Stripping off everything but my shorts, I plunged straight into the warm waters of the Caribbean. I was so hot that I would have preferred the cold English Channel, but I could hardly complain. I left my complaints for when I returned to the beach. Someone had kindly relieved me of all of my running gear. I could hardly believe it; there was nobody else around. I stood there looking up and down the beach just in case I had come ashore in the wrong place. A quiet and empty beach confirmed my worst fears. I would now have to walk back in my very short and very scruffy shorts. My only consolation was that at least I had not been tempted to go skinny dipping. Walking into the elegant hotel lobby, I tried to look as inconspicuous as possible as I queued up to get a replacement room key. The trail of sand and water behind me gave everyone a clue as to why I was standing there in just a pair of wet running shorts. The only bright side was that my acute embarrassment made me forget all about the heat exhaustion.

Fast forward a few years, and we were staying at the Tradewinds Hotel at the top of Dickenson Bay. This lovely boutique hotel was solely for British Airways crews. I expect our previous hotel wanted to avoid any more semi-naked pilots scaring their guests and making a mess of their lobby. On this trip, I had with me my very good friend and the illustrator of my first two books, Mike McCarthy. Mike was, at the time, a fireman. In fact, he was the head of a county fire service. Mike is well over six feet tall and wore a very iffy 1970s moustache. Rumours were rife when the crew discovered that we were there together and he was sharing my room. Luckily, our respective wives had fully approved of the boys-only tour.

We walked halfway down the steep hill to the excellent Pari Pizza restaurant on the first night. We all enjoyed far too much to eat and drink. Mike especially, enjoyed himself as humorously, he fended off questions about his relationship with me. It was all done with great humour. Eventually, we staggered back up the hill to have a very ill-advised nightcap.

The following day, we both woke up with a well-deserved headache. My usual remedy was to run a hangover off, and I informed Mike of my intentions. To my surprise, he insisted on coming with me. I tried to dissuade him; we had overslept, and it was now mid-morning and scorching. Whilst I was used to running in the heat, Mike was not. He was fit, but his last run in the sun had been a few years ago, and Bognor Regis on the Sussex coast was not well known for temperature extremes.

On top of that, the last part of the run was up the very long and steep hill back to the hotel we had climbed the previous night. Forty minutes later, Mike and I were climbing this hill in the midday sun. I could see that Mike was really struggling, and I suggested we stop and walk the rest of the way.

Mike was made of sterner stuff and kept reminding me that real firemen never gave up. I had never thought of him as a real fireman but thought this was not the time to mention that. Although I believe he had once watched real firefighters at work, he was now a Senior District Officer. This was about as important as a firefighter could be. In other words, he sat behind a desk and made important decisions, a fact I kept reminding him of. The banter continued until we came around a very steep bend and passed Pari Pizza, the scene of our downfall the previous night.

Well, that was it for Mike. The smell of freshly baked pizza and beer was the final straw. Mixed with the onset of heat exhaustion, poor Mike leaned against a tree in the car park and duly returned the pizza he had eaten the night before. The remainder of the run was very sedate. I only mentioned once or twice that Pari Pizza did not accept returns. I also mentioned it a few times during the rest of our trip. Poor Mike was so traumatised, he even shaved off his dubious moustache, a decision that upset his wife when we returned home. Mike and I have never run together since then. Although we are still great friends, I can never see us repeating a pizza run again.

Chapter 8

Hot and High and Freezing

An interesting thing about being a long-haul airline pilot and a runner is that literally one day, you could be running in snow; the next, you could be running in the heat at eight thousand feet above sea level. Your poor old body has no time to adapt to the different extremes, and you end up just getting on with it.

I was in Chicago and running alongside Lake Michigan. Unknowingly, I was also running into an approaching snowstorm. I was neither prepared nor dressed for the weather I was about to encounter. It was only early October, not usually a time of year when I would expect such harsh conditions. We had landed at O'Hare International Airport only a few hours previously. It was a sunny afternoon, and the temperature was a pleasant ten degrees, with no hint of what was to come. We were staying at the wonderfully named Knickerbocker Hotel.

This was situated just off the Golden Mile in the heart of the city. It was, however, only a five-minute run down to an underpass, and from there, you were on a beautiful lakeside path. Once on this path, I set off for a golf course some three miles distant. I wore just a thin vest and shorts, my usual running attire, even in the winter. The forecast was for the possibility of light snow later that night and the following day, which was difficult to believe in the current conditions. Thirty minutes later, the sun had disappeared behind some of the darkest clouds I had ever seen. The temperature dropped as the sun was swallowed by these dark aerial mountains of cumulonimbus clouds. It was like suddenly stepping into a giant freezer. I could not believe how quickly the weather had changed. One moment sunshine; the next, semi-darkness and freezing temperatures. And then, the lake-effect snowstorm arrived.

For those of you, like me, who have never encountered lake-effect snow, it is an incredible experience. Cold air moves down from Canada and reaches the relatively warm waters of the Great Lakes. This warms the lower part of the cloud, which then collects the moisture from the lake and rises into the atmosphere. As it rises, it cools quickly, and the moisture turns into snow. And my God, does it snow! One moment, I was running along quite happily, looking ahead for the approaching turning point at the golf course. Suddenly, I was thrown into a giant freezer, and someone was throwing snow in my face. Visibility went from almost unlimited to virtually zero. Squinting ahead, I could see that the path I was following was rapidly disappearing as the snow settled. It was definitely time to turn back. Unfortunately, I was now about five kilometres from the warmth of the hotel. As the temperature continued dropping, my head and hands began to suffer. Of course, I had no hat or gloves; that would have been far too sensible. I decided to head towards the main road as I could no longer even make out the lakeside path.

Obviously, everyone else in Chicago had been prepared for this turn of events as the few people brave enough to be out all seemed to be suitably dressed in warm clothing. I received curious stares as I shivered along the snow-covered pavements. The only sensible thing I had done before leaving my hotel room was to put a crisp twenty-dollar note in my pocket for any unexpected emergencies. This was now one of those. I was beginning to get frostbite. I lost all feeling in my hands and had a pounding headache. I needed to buy a woolly hat and gloves and buy them quickly. Salvation appeared to be at hand as a shop selling both items appeared in the whiteout. I did not need any encouragement and stepped into the warm interior with a massive sigh of relief. I stood in the entrance shaking off the snow like a sheepdog after a few hours of playing in the fields. Only a few customers were in the shop, but they all turned around to see what would emerge when all this snow was finally discarded.

Feeling very self-conscious, I made my way to the rows of hats and gloves. After a couple of moments, I realised I could only afford a hat or some gloves. My meagre twenty dollars would not stretch to both. Now, this was a very interesting dilemma. Which part of my anatomy would I sacrifice, and which would I keep? Fingers are handy, and as I stood there, I could think of lots of things that I would be unable to do if I lost a few. The list seemed endless, but in the end, my head won the day. Well, I did only have one, and although, like today, it did not always work very well, I could not imagine life without it. So, I clutched the warmest woolly hat I could afford and made my way to the checkout counter. I laid my precious purchase before the shop assistant and offered up my solitary note. Suddenly, I realised that the few people in the shop were all looking at me. I wanted to get out of there as quickly as possible and return to the warmth of my hotel room. The elderly gentleman serving me gave me one of those looks, the one that says, "are you crazy?" Funnily enough, I have received many of those looks over the years.

Then, he asked me if I knew just how unwise it was to go out in conditions like these without proper protection. I replied that I was British, which seemed to explain everything he needed to know. I received another look; this one was more sympathetic than judgemental. He insisted that I needed both a hat and gloves, not just a hat. I explained that I only had twenty dollars with me and had just flown in from London a few hours ago. I was unsure of the relevance of that last piece of information; it just popped out. The shop assistant came around from behind the counter, and for a second, I thought he was going to throw me out. Instead, he walked slowly over to the display of hats and gloves and began studying the garments. He returned with a different hat, much more substantial than the one I had chosen, and a warm pair of gloves. He placed both items on the counter in front of me. I started to explain again that I only had twenty dollars with me, and these items cost over sixty.

What followed next was one of the kindest deeds I have ever encountered. The shopkeeper displayed complete faith in the character of a total stranger. He explained that my safety was more important than money. I was more than welcome to return and pay the balance; if not, I could consider the excess a gift. And with that, he took my twenty dollars and wished me well with the rest of my run. Suitably attired, I ran the last few kilometres in relative comfort; it is surprising just what a difference a hat and gloves can make.

The next day, the snowstorm had passed as quickly as it had arrived. The temperature had risen slightly, and although it was still cold, it was a beautiful day for a run. I had felt so indebted the previous day to the old gentleman who had helped me that I couldn't return quickly enough. I had the money in my pocket to pay the balance I owed. As I entered the shop, I hoped that the same assistant would be there today. I hated the thought that he would be in trouble for his kindness. Looking around, I could see no sign of my saviour. I asked the female assistant if the elderly gentleman who had served me yesterday was working today? She looked at me with a puzzled expression on her face. Apparently, they had no elderly assistants. I tried to offer the forty dollars I owed, but she informed me that she could not accept my money without knowing what it was for. Then, she wandered off to find the manager.

I stood waiting. Had I come to the wrong shop? Looking around, there was the display of hats and gloves that I had seen the day before. I was definitely in the right place.

The assistant returned with the manager, another lady, definitely not the old gentleman from the previous day. I repeated my story and again, tried to pay what I owed. I was asked to describe who had served me. Suddenly, there was a glimmer of understanding in the manager's eyes. She explained that I had been helped by the shop's owner. He only came in about once a month, and his bookkeeping was atrocious. He rarely put items through the system correctly, giving their accountant many headaches. She did, however, inform me that he rarely gave anything away. He was very careful with that sort of thing. If he had given me the hat and gloves for twenty dollars, then that's what he wanted for them. And anyway, if she tried to put the extra money through the system today, the accountant would not thank her. I left the shop with my money in my pocket, but my faith in human kindness was overflowing. I always try to make sure I never leave on a run without the proper clothing. Sadly, it's not a promise to myself that I always keep.

Two days later, I woke up in my hotel room, this time in Mexico City and a very different world. All memories of ice and snow melted quickly as I looked out of my hotel window at the heat haze that distorted the scene below. Earlier that morning, we had flown in from London, a long and tiring flight. Mexico City sits in the Valley of Mexico and is surrounded by towering volcanoes. The city is nearly eight thousand feet above sea level, and you have a very challenging environment for both an aircraft and a runner.

The approach that morning had been a difficult one. The arrival involved flying along a narrow corridor to avoid the high peaks and mountains around the city. However, at this time of the year, massive thunderstorms would completely envelop our arrival route. We would not only have to fly around the mountains but also avoid the worst of the weather. Communication with air traffic was difficult as the controllers spoke only very basic English and communications with all the local traffic were in Spanish. That morning's approach and landing were even more difficult as we had shut down one of the aircraft's engines. Even the mighty Boeing 747 had performance problems flying on three engines when the airport was so high. After all that excitement, I decided sleep was more appropriate than a quick run.

The following day, as I was putting on my running gear, I was about to discover that I was also susceptible to the lack of oxygen at this height. My performance, like the Jumbo's, was hampered by the city's altitude.

Mexico City is a cauldron of humanity, vehicles, noise and pollution, mixed together in an inland basin. A large part of the city had been built on a lakebed drained long ago. As I stepped out into the afternoon sunshine, all these factors overwhelmed my senses simultaneously. 'Can I run in these conditions?' I thought to myself, as the only car in the city that was not blaring its horn suddenly realised its omission and joined in the cacophony of noise.

Directly outside the hotel stood the beautiful Angel of Independence statue. High on her plinth, the golden Angel was situated on a roundabout in the city's main avenue. She was pointing to something in the distance, so I decided to go and find out what this majestic Angel was pointing at. The avenue itself was just as beautiful. It was wide and divided in two by a line of magnificent trees. Despite the vast volume of traffic, the avenue had maintained its splendour. There was plenty of room along the equally wide pavement for me to run without hindrance. I set off at a conservative pace. I had heard about the problems of high-altitude running, and I wanted to avoid over-exerting myself and running out of puff before exploring this fascinating place.

As I made my way along this thoroughfare, I began to appreciate the problems that the Jumbo had in this rarefied atmosphere. Your heart, or engines if you are a 747, needed more oxygen than the air could supply. This lack of oxygen will quickly become a big problem if an allowance is not made. If I tried to take off at the maximum aircraft weight in Mexico, the Jumbo would not get airborne. Whilst we could easily lift three hundred and ninety tonnes off the runway in London, we had to drastically reduce our weight to get airborne from Mexico City. The same applied to my body. If I set off at my usual pace, I would very quickly come to a stop. Of course, the human body, being more intelligent than an aircraft, can eventually adapt by creating more oxygen-carrying red blood cells. However, this took time which is why serious athletes spent weeks in high-altitude training. I was not a serious athlete, and so I did the only thing open to me, I slowed down.

Twenty minutes later, I was still running well, albeit at this new reduced pace. I was rewarded by the sight of two massive iron gates, which marked the entrance to the awe-inspiring Chapultepec Park.

I had never heard of this park before I ran between these two magnificent gates and started to run up the many flights of stairs towards the start of the park. On this occasion, I was very fortunate; unbeknown to me, the day was a national holiday celebrating Mexico's Independence. Everywhere I looked, there were stalls selling just about anything you could think of. The sounds, sights and smells were mixed with the noise of children's laughter. Carnival was definitely in town. Whilst this made for a beautiful sight, it did little to help with my run. It was impossible to run through the crowds, so I prepared to turn around and leave the park. To my right, I noticed a fellow runner disappear down a small path, and so, of course, I followed.

The path wound through the woodland that surrounded the park. One moment, I had been running along a major highway, and now, I found myself in the urban countryside; it was magical.

The runner I had seen was part of a group of military cadets, obviously out on a training run before doing other military things that soldiers do. I had now caught up with this runner. There were probably about twenty soldiers running along two abreast. I thought I was running slowly, but these guys seemed to be taking it really easy. Maybe, they had had a hard morning shooting things, but they certainly were in no hurry to get to their next assignment. I hate overtaking anyone, no matter where in the world you are; if you run up behind someone on a narrow path, you will scare the hell out of them. People somehow enter their own world while walking or running in remote places. As I pound up behind them, I try to make each step as loud as possible to warn them of my approach. If this does not work, which it usually does not, I try a few loud coughs. As I get close, I have to resort to calling out, "Excuse Me."

It is incredible what impact these two simple, innocuous words can have on an unsuspecting victim. Everyone, without exception, will jump. They could never have envisaged that there could be someone so close behind them and that someone may want to overtake them. The mildest form of this kind of shock is a little jump in the air, a startled look, and an apology for being in the way. Other people will make involuntary noises as suddenly, they realise that they are not alone in the world. Others will raise their arms, ready to defend themselves. The more elderly will accept their fate and prepare to die. The variations are endless, and the only common theme is that I end up feeling dreadful at inflicting so much distress on an unsuspecting public.

My overtaking adventures were about to rise to new heights. Initially, I had held back and followed the group of soldiers at a safe distance. I remembered that this was my first run at such a height, and I did not want to run out of steam so far away from the hotel. However, I was feeling really well. I had a lot of energy and wanted to continue running at my original pace. The guys in front were a lot slower than me. I needed to get past them. I considered my options. I could hang back and wait for the path to divide or get wider. I could turn around and try to find another point at which to pass. Or I could stamp my feet, cough loudly, and start shouting, "Excuse Me," in Spanish. By now, you probably know me well enough to guess which option I chose.

As I started to accelerate towards the rear runners, I tried to think of the Spanish equivalent of 'Excuse me'. Nothing came to mind, so I reverted to every English tourist's idea of speaking the local language. I put on a funny accent and added a few vowels to the end of each word.

The first of the two soldiers heard stamping and coughing. Then something like "Excuseea." To me, this sounded very much like it could be the Spanish version of excuse me.

From their reaction, it must have sounded very much like, "Beware, I am going to inflict a horrible death on you." I suppose to be fair; it did sound a little like 'Execute'. Both not only jumped a few feet in the air, they managed to twist around in mid-air and attempt to reach for their non-existent guns. Obviously, they had forgotten their weapon training earlier that day. They literally fell to the wayside as they tried to recover from the shock. I was now behind the next pair of runners. 'My God, I hoped none of them had a weapon, as this could get interesting', I thought. I reverted to my best English accent as politely, I called out a warning that I was about to overtake them. Their reaction was even more extreme than my first two victims. This time, one fell over, and the other, thinking he was under attack, ran away into the woods. 'No medals for bravery were on his horizon', I thought to myself.

By this time, the remainder of the troop realised they were under immediate threat and went into a well-rehearsed drill to deal with such a dilemma. They all ran into the woods. I could hardly believe the pandemonium I had caused with my overtaking protocol. Did I stop and apologise to these poor recruits, or did I run as fast as possible, get off the path, and lose myself in the crowds? Again, I think you know me well enough to guess which route I took. Less than thirty minutes later, I puffed and panted back into the hotel's reception area. The heat and the high altitude had finally caught up with me, and I was exhausted as I collapsed onto my bed.

I had learnt three valuable lessons from my adventure that afternoon. Mexico City was an incredible place. Hot and high-altitude running is very tough on the body. And finally, if you want to invade Mexico, run up behind their army and shout "Excuse Me," in Spanglish.

Chapter 9

To Run or Not To Run? That is the Question

My first experience of this amazing country, India, was in the mid-1980s. We were on the approach to Mumbai, or Bombay, as it was then known. Incredibly, the first thing that alerted you to the fact that you were approaching India would be the intoxicating aroma slowly wafting into the flight deck. Occasionally, before you could even see the runway, the sweet smell of spices and the not-so-sweet aroma of pollution would be the first indication that you were about to land in India. Due to this pollution and high temperatures, the visibility as we landed was always poor and sometimes non-existent. The endless flow of traffic beneath us belched out vast quantities of thick black smoke. There were no checks on emissions in those days. This, mixed with the numerous roadside fires and industrial waste, made the air quality so poor that the smell would be sucked in by the aircraft's air conditioning system as we descended below a thousand feet. Over the coming decades, I would learn to love this early introduction to India. However, at this point, India had yet to seduce me, and I felt somewhat wary of this vast and strange new place.

That first drive from the airport to the hotel took forever. Although it was still very early in the morning, the roads and pavements were crammed with a plethora of people, vehicles, and animals. Cows are considered sacred in India and have an absolute right of way. Basically, these beasts could go anywhere they wanted. Imagine a busy motorway with a few cows wandering between the lanes. You will then have a good idea of what to expect in India. As we inched slowly through this melee, I tried to imagine how I could run through such chaos. Little did I know it then, but I would still have the same doubts four decades later. As I stared out of the window of the crew bus, I imagined that running in this strange land would be challenging, to say the least.

Everything about India seemed strange and exotic. We were met at the hotel by Sikh guards, fully attired in their ceremonial outfits. The hotel contrasted completely with the chaos outside. It was exquisite, colossal, and palatial. It was more of a seven than a five-star establishment. The whole building felt more like a palace than a hotel. Bellhops, resplendent in their red uniforms and pillbox hats, rushed to relieve me of my briefcase. A tray with glasses of freshly squeezed fruit juice was placed before me as I arrived at the reception desk. 'I could get used to this', I thought to myself as a receptionist offered me a cool towel to wipe my brow. Even my room was more like an apartment than a hotel room. Gratefully, I sank onto the most enormous bed I had ever seen. India had exhausted me, and I hadn't even set foot outside yet.

I awoke six hours later and started putting on my running gear. Pulling back the huge curtains, I squinted out into the bright sunshine. I reflected on this luxury as I looked out of my window at the scene below me. I was in my ivory tower, looking down at some of the worst deprivation I had ever witnessed. Below was a sprawling mass of cardboard and corrugated iron huts. They were crammed together amidst mountains of rubbish. There were open sewer pipes alongside which young, very young, children played. I could hardly believe my eyes. How could there be such a stark contrast within such a short distance? The sheer inequality of the situation struck me like a slap in the face. Stunned, I sat back on my bed as if I had been pushed roughly by an invisible hand. I felt a mixture of sadness, guilt, and regret. All thoughts of going for a run were pushed to the back of my mind. Did I have the courage to face the inhumanity and poverty I had just witnessed through the windows of this luxurious gilded cage?

Thirty minutes later, I had recovered enough to decide I could not stay in my room. I had to go running; after all, it's what I did. As I walked through the dazzling front lobby, all eyes turned to watch this scruffy individual in shorts and a vest make his way to the front entrance. As I passed through the magnificent door, the Sikh guards again turned to salute. Both their hands rose halfway up towards their foreheads and froze in mid-air. Neither was quite sure what to say or do. This was not a sight they were used to in the hotel's resplendent front lobby. I imagined they were ready to evict this scruffy individual as they stepped forward, blocking my way. Almost instantly, their demeanour changed as they recognised me from my arrival that morning. Their hands shot up in a friendly salute, and a greeting of "Good afternoon, captain," replaced their stern looks.

Returning their greeting, I set off down the long hotel driveway and out into the unknown. The hotel was set on its vast grounds like a sea of tranquillity set amid a vast storm. The distance from the hotel lobby to the main road outside was no more than five hundred metres, yet it was like travelling across continents; such was the contrast. The first few minutes of my run were along a beautifully manicured path lined with trees and shrubs. Birds sang, and peacocks wandered across the perfectly manicured lawns. Sprinkler systems kept the whole scene dewy in the searing heat. To my right, I could glimpse a colossal swimming pool complete with an outside bar and restaurant. Happy couples sat at the pool bar sipping afternoon cocktails. 'This was paradise on earth', I thought to myself; my spirits rose, and some of my earlier doubts and reservations disappeared, although sadly, not for long.

I reached the main gated entrance to the hotel through which we had driven in the early morning darkness. Four heavily armed security guards stood by the barrier, checking everyone who entered and left the hotel complex. I waited patiently for them to lift the barrier to allow me through. Instead of the barrier rising, two guards approached and asked me what I was doing and why I was leaving the hotel. This surprised me, especially when they wanted to know my room number. Also, they demanded my name and when I had checked into the hotel. I half expected them to ask what I had for breakfast and to know my inside leg measurements. They were not rude, but they made it clear that they were suspicious of me. It was the last straw when I explained that I was going to run in forty degrees of heat. Instructing me to stay where I was, one of the guards returned to his hut. I could see him making a very animated phone call, I assumed, to the hotel's reception desk. The guard returned with an apology and quickly explained to his friend that I was British. That seemed an entirely acceptable reason for me wanting to go running where apparently, no runner had ventured before. They lifted the barrier with a warning to take care and not to give the street beggars any money. I was free and feeling a little like a character from *The Great Escape*. Quickly, I took advantage of my newfound freedom and accelerated down the street.

As I drew away from the hotel, I began to appreciate the extremes India can throw at you, often in a matter of moments.

The traffic noise was intense and overpowering. Obviously, not one of the vehicles had an exhaust. Ancient lorries spewed out trails of thick black smoke, so thick that you could taste black tar as it hit the back of your throat. The traffic was bad enough. I had experienced a sample of what to expect on the drive from the airport. What I had not expected, nor was prepared for, was the sheer volume of humanity that engulfed me as I left the hotel grounds. There were people literally everywhere. The pavements were overrun by a tsunami of humanity. Everyone seemed in a desperate hurry to be somewhere else. From the youngest child to very old men and women, all seemed desperate to be elsewhere. Children as young as four or five darted in and out of the speeding traffic as they crossed a six-lane highway. To add to the chaos, stray dogs yelped and barked as they attempted to avoid human and automotive traffic. I had never seen anything like it, and literally, it stopped me in my tracks as I caught one of my feet in the numerous potholes scattered along the pavement and roads.

Just like Times Square on New Year's Eve, everyone and everything seemed to be going in all directions at the same time. How this kaleidoscope of movement and noise did not collapse in on itself baffled me. Well, it would have baffled me if I had had time to think about it. Instead, I ended up face down in a crumpled heap. Once again, I had failed to recover from a stumble and was paying the painful price.

Falling over is part of running. Go running, and eventually, you will trip over something and end up face-down on the ground. If you are really unlucky, you may end up in something deeply unpleasant. This time, I was really unlucky. It's just a fact of a runner's life. Usually, everyone will stop and stare at this comical scene. Not in India. Nobody looked, stared or even noticed as this strange foreigner lay prone on the pavement. They just walked around, over and occasionally on me as I struggled to my feet and tried to regain some dignity. Wiping away some of the blood running down my left leg, I set off again, this time paying more attention to where I placed my feet rather than what was happening around me. This new tactic worked for about thirty seconds, and then, I found myself face down on the pavement again. 'This run was not going to plan', I thought to myself, as I spat out another mouthful of Bombay dirt. Shaking the dust and grime away and now tending to the blood flowing liberally down both legs, I made a vow to myself that I managed to keep for the remainder of my career. Indian cities are not places for me to run in.

I stood looking around me, true to form; nobody seemed to have noticed my new calamity. Did I return to the hotel, or should I consider exploring this amazing place solely by walking? That afternoon, I began a tradition that I was to continue for over thirty years. I merely gave up on the idea of running in Indian cities. Quite simply, it was too dangerous. The condition of the pavements and roads made it impossible to run without falling over. However, I did not want to just stroll around and return to the hotel. I had a few rupees in my pocket, so I decided to walk until I could walk no further. Then, I would wave down a tuk-tuk for the journey back to the hotel. These fantastic three-wheeled contraptions were absolutely everywhere. Their yellow and black markings made them look like a swarm of wasps as they surged through the traffic. You just had to raise your hand, and they flocked to you, again like wasps to jam sandwiches. A quick barter on the price, and you were on your way.

Buses and cars were completely ignored as the tuk-tuk driver would do an about-turn in the middle of the traffic and drive down a motorway on the wrong side of the road. This deathly manoeuvre was designed to save a few precious seconds or to be the first to pick up a prospective passenger. They scared the hell out of me, but I loved every second I spent in those tuk-tuks. I clung to them as though they were my last moments on earth, which, to be fair, occasionally, they very nearly were. Without realising it, I had begun my love affair with India. However, I was on my first expedition into the heart of the city. What I was about to see and experience was not the ideal start to any relationship. Having realised that running these streets was impossible, I settled for second best and set off to walk through Bombay.

Quite quickly, I found my way into the settlement I had seen from my hotel room. From the street level, the scene was even more upsetting. The smell from the open sewers was overwhelming, and I gagged as the acrid odour attacked my senses. I turned my head away instinctively as I started to gag on the overpowering smell of human excrement. Trying to avoid breathing in too deeply, which in stifling heat is always tricky, I looked around this vast cardboard and corrugated iron habitation. I felt myself tense as suddenly, I realised that I had wandered too far from the main street. Looking around me, it was apparent that I was the only European.

I have been blessed with a good sense of self-preservation, and now all my senses were screaming at me. Realising I could be in extreme danger, I turned around and tried to find the quickest escape route. It was a huge mistake. To my horror, I noticed that my presence in this community had not gone unnoticed. There, standing directly behind me, were at least twenty faces glaring at me. Each face seemed to be shouting or screaming something I did not understand. I knew that I could not run away. I had already tried running and discovered that it was simply impossible. My 'Fight or Flight' options were seriously reduced. If I were going to get out of this alive, I would have to fight. However, the odds of at least twenty to one did not bode well for my chances. My hands had, without my noticing, already turned into fists. I guess my body was entering the fight stage all by itself.

With little hope of survival, I faced the mob. I was as ready as I would ever be. Although I knew that it would not end well for me, I stood my ground and awaited my fate. The first few assailants ran at me, shouting and waving their arms. I looked at their faces, trying to understand how I could have provoked such anger. Had I committed some heinous religious blasphemy that could only be punished by death? I guessed I would never find out as the first few hands grabbed me.

As I raised my arms to protect my face, I could, at last, understand what they were shouting, "Cricket, cricket, cricket, Botham, Botham, Botham." This was interspersed with shouts of "Tendulkar, Tendulkar, Tendulkar."

These, mostly teenage boys, had somehow mistaken me for one of the visiting England cricketers. I was not about to be beaten to death. I was being swamped by a crowd of cricket fans. I was a hero, not a villain. I just hoped they would still think that when I told them I was only the pilot of the aircraft that had brought the England cricket team to India, not one of the players. On second thoughts, I decided to keep that little gem to myself. Why spoil their day or mine? Despite their evident poverty, the majority spoke good English and seemed bright and full of life.

There was, and sadly still is, a terrible and pervading process of begging on the streets of Mumbai and Delhi. Desperately young children are groomed to beg. The younger, the better. Criminals would literally buy these children from families who could not afford to feed them and then send them out to beg. They were beaten if they did not bring in enough money at the end of the day. There were horrendous stories of babies being deliberately disabled by tying their arms and legs into unnatural positions. Consequently, they grew up into grossly disfigured children. Apparently, they earned more money than non-disabled children.

Thank God the children in the crowd in front of me were all fit and healthy, apart from being painfully thin. Not one of them asked for a single rupee. All they wanted to do was talk about cricket. Quickly, I learned that their passion for the game is on par with the English love for football. So, for these people having me in their midst was similar to David Beckham walking into a housing estate in Manchester.

I answered each question as best I could, without revealing my true identity. My answers, however, were becoming vaguer and vaguer. I noticed that some of my crowd had started to drift away, so I did my best to drift with them. To this day, I wonder if some of those youngsters still believed they had met an international cricketer. For all I know, they might still be telling their grandchildren of the day the great Ian Botham came to visit them. As is customary with Indian cricket, they beat England easily as the great batsman, Tendulkar, destroyed the English bowling attack. As for me, I dined out on the story for longer than I should have.

I continued walking around Indian cities for the next thirty-four years. I learnt to carry a lot of small rupee notes to hand out to the children begging. I learnt very quickly that giving a beggar a large amount of money would seal his fate, and the other beggars would attack him and take the money. Ten rupees was just the right amount, enough to make the beggar happy but not enough for the others to turn on him. Not once in all those years did I again feel in any danger. Yes, begging children could be considered a nuisance. Still, I always thought about how lucky my two young sons were compared to these sad and lonely youngsters with absolutely nothing. Gladly, I produced note after note, even though I was aware that the money was going mainly to criminal gangs. However, if it stopped that child from being beaten that day, that was good enough for me.

Despite all my walking through the city, I still had withdrawal symptoms from being unable to run. I needed to get my running fix and get it fast. And so, I resorted to that dreaded, unedifying contraption known as the treadmill or running machine.

These heinous devices could normally be found in the basements of all the hotels we stayed in. They were located in the gyms, again a place that filled me with dread. However, in India, I had no choice. It was either the running machine or not running at all. You can guess which option I chose.

I approached these machines with a wary eye. I looked at the other runners. There were about ten of these torture devices lined up in a row. Each runner looked like a gerbil running on a continuous, monotonous wheel, never getting anywhere. I had to wait my turn, so I tried the various, equally tortuous weightlifting machines. Everyone I looked at seemed super fit, with muscles everywhere. The men also looked seriously toned as well! It was humiliating to sit on a machine and try to lift the same weights the previous occupier had just effortlessly pumped up and down for the last ten minutes. The chagrin of getting up and removing half of the weights to begin my workout was mortifying. Over the years, I managed to devise a suitable strategy that worked splendidly. Instead of trying to lift the weights left by the last person, I would adjust the weights, which were usually at the back of the machine. I could have been adding weights, not taking them off. I would remove enough weight so as not to embarrass myself. After lifting these paperweights up and down twenty times, I went to the back of the machine once more. Once there, I added weight after weight until I was satisfied that only Hercules could manage such a load. I would move on to the next machine and repeat the process.

Then, I would sit and watch the next person trying to use the machine I had just vacated. Everyone likes to feel the weights lifted by the previous occupant. I would sit and watch as they grabbed the bars or ropes and began to pull or push. Of course, nothing happened. They simply could not move it an inch. They would look at me with renewed respect. I responded with a shrug of my shoulders which I hoped translated as, "You too could be like me if you try hard enough."

Smiling inside, I noticed that one of the running machines was now available. Dropping my weights in a rush to get to the free machine, I forgot to add more weights as I left my machine. I was mortified when a slightly built lady sat down and almost pulled the ropes off the machine. I could see her starting to add weight after weight. I was too embarrassed to see how many she added. Anyway, it was time to run; I was good at running. What could possibly go wrong?

As I mentioned earlier, the gym was in the basement of our beautiful hotel. It was a large and very well-equipped establishment. As the gym was subterranean, there was no natural light. However, the bright lights and vast mirrors on the walls more than compensated for this. These were interspersed with large wall murals so that the vainer of the participants could admire themselves as they worked out. I stepped onto my running machine and tried to determine what the knobs and buttons did. This was not my first time on one of these revolving drive belt wonders, but it was undoubtedly the first time I could plug in my earphones and watch television whilst I ran.

There is a definite art to running on a machine. You must understand that the ground beneath you is moving, not yourself. Whilst this seems pretty obvious when you are not on the machine, it does take a while for the brain to realise what is going on once you mount the beast. My method of coping was to start slowly at ten kilometres an hour, and as I got used to the rhythm, I gradually increased the pace. As I hated these damn machines, my plan was always to run as fast as I could for as short a period as I could. Ten kilometres was my limit, and I often got off at five because I hated this type of running. Also, I was slightly afraid that a giant hand would reach out and put me back in my hamster cage.

And so today, I started out slowly, as usual. However, after my embarrassment in the weightlifting area, I was keen to return to my room, shower and go for a beer. I set my distance limit to just five kilometres and set the pace to the maximum, something I rarely did. With my earphones attached, I ran my heart out. A large mirror was on the wall about two feet in front of the machine. I was sweating heavily and watching the time and distance increase on the machine's dials. I was doing well. Only another kilometre to go. I was running at my maximum pace, even slightly above it. Everything went so well until all the lights went out, including mine.

As I mentioned, on a running machine, the road or band beneath you moves, and you effectively stay stationary. When, however, the road suddenly stops moving, the process is reversed. The road stands still, and you, the runner, move forward. If you are running as fast as possible during this unexpected role reversal, things can get out of hand very quickly.

The running machine had stopped dead, but I, of course, hadn't. I went straight over the front of the machine at sixteen kilometres an hour. Then, I collided with the mirror I had been admiring myself in only moments earlier. I slid down the gap between the device and the wall like a discarded sack of potatoes. Calamitously, I performed this manoeuvre headfirst and became wedged upside down in the small space between the wall and the machine. Added to this, my head had, with some impact, bounced off the wall, making clear thinking almost impossible. I hung there for a few moments trying to work out what had just happened. It was completely dark, with not a flicker of light anywhere. I was totally disoriented. Maybe, I had been in a giant hamster's cage after all. Struggle as I might, I could not free myself. My fingertips could just about touch the ground but not with sufficient purchase to push myself up and back over the machine. I was there for the duration. I just hoped the lights would turn on before I became unconscious. It was so dark that maybe I had already passed out? Suddenly and thankfully, the world I knew was once again bathed in bright fluorescent light.

It took two of the gym instructors to pull me out of that inverted world. As they tugged at my running shorts to pull me backwards, whatever little dignity I had left vanished along with half of my shorts. Eventually, when they freed me, I could see a small group from the weightlifting area watching with interest. The slight lady who had taken over my last weightlifting machine had a large grin on her face. As far as she was concerned, I had got what I deserved. A little part of me had to agree with her.

Despite all of this, India and her people still and will forever hold me in their spell. I just wish they would look after their children and stray dogs with much more compassion. Oh, and maybe, fill in all those potholes.

Chapter 10

Magnificent, Beautiful and Scary

My first experience of Africa was when I was five years old. We were on a family holiday in Gibraltar and decided to take a ferry across to Tangiers. I had been asking my parents about the country I could see across the Straits of Gibraltar. The mountains in the distance seemed to dwarf the rock we were staying on. I had childlike visions of a new and exotic land, unlike anything I had ever seen before. After a few days of pleading, finally, I found myself on an old ferry spewing out vast quantities of black, oily smoke as it made its way lazily towards this vast new continent. I was on my way to Africa. That five-year-old boy could never have imagined the fun, excitement and terror this land would bring him over the next six decades. As I stepped off the boat that day, I was overwhelmed by the sights, smells, and commotion surrounding me. I have rarely experienced such fascination before or since. Yet even my young mind realised that behind the colours and buzzing activity, there lurked a dark side to this wonderful place. My love-hate relationship with Africa was about to begin.

Fast forward a few decades, and you find me on my first flight on the Boeing 747. I am a junior first officer, flying the approach and landing at Nairobi Airport. Kenya is a beautiful country, lying on the eastern side of the continent. The city itself is some six thousand feet above sea level. The air is very thin, made more noticeable by the usually high temperatures. This makes the handling of the aircraft more complicated. The aeroplane becomes very slippery as it cuts through the thinner air. The pilot, especially a pilot brand new to the Jumbo, has to think much further ahead than usual. It is essential to slow the aircraft down a lot earlier than normal. At the same time, you have to avoid the Ngong hills. Then there is a sharp turn to the left to fly down the valley towards the runway. Certainly, I had my hands full, attempting my first-ever landing on the 747. As I was about to be reminded that day, this thin air also affects the human body as I set off on another first, my first run in Africa.

In the early morning mist, we had touched down, or to be brutally honest, bumped down. Finally, I had successfully achieved my first 747 landing. After a long drive to the hotel in downtown Nairobi, I tried to get a few hours of sleep. The long debrief from the training captain was still ringing in my ears as I tried to clear my mind and rest after the long night flight. Was I ever going to be able to tame this beast of an aircraft?

Finally giving up on the hope of any rest, I climbed out of bed and slowly and methodically began my usual ritual of putting on my running gear. I had agreed to a game of golf later that day, and I wanted to get my run out of the way in plenty of time to meet the captain. If my landing had upset him, I hated to think of what he would say about my golf. I just prayed that I would not embarrass myself with an air shot, something that was an occasional part of my game. Banishing these thoughts, I made my way downstairs and into the lobby of the Inter-Continental Hotel.

I had looked at a very basic map of the area; no mobile phones or GPS in the 1980s. There appeared to be an open area opposite the hotel named Uhuru Park. In my mind, I envisaged a sort of Central Park in New York. In reality, I was about to discover that the park, certainly when I first visited, was not a place for a very naive foreigner.

Going through the revolving doors of the hotel entrance, I realised that running in this vast and busy city would be more complex than I had hoped. Firstly, the heat was overpowering, but I was expecting that, and to be honest, I did not mind running in hot climates. Secondly, the pavements were overflowing with pedestrians, animals and, worst of all, young children wandering the streets, begging for food scraps. This was something I had not been expecting.

I soon realised that, as in India, running the streets of Nairobi would be difficult, if not impossible. However, there was the promise of a park run close by; if only I could navigate the chaotic motorway between me and the park. I set off to find a bridge to cross this eight-lane monster. There was no way I would risk playing dodgems with the traffic as many of the locals were doing.

As I made my way from the hotel, I realised that I would have great difficulty getting to the park, let alone running around it. In India, the sheer multitude of humanity was the main obstacle to running. The problem here was that everyone I ran into wanted something from me. They either wanted me to buy something from them, or to give them something. Occasionally, they wanted both at the same time.

Now, being English, the most commonly used word when we are abroad is, "Sorry." I was either apologising for not wanting to buy something or not having any money to give them.

However, I really began to appreciate the meaning of the word sorry when I recognised how many young children appeared to be living on the streets. Whereas I could run past vendors and beggars, I found it impossible to run past these little lost souls. A sudden yearning to help overwhelmed me. How on earth could a country allow such adversity to go apparently unnoticed? I had been running for less than ten minutes, and in that time, I had seen so many abandoned children. There was nothing I could do to help as I passed them by. I had no money on me. I decided to continue my run, but then I would return, bringing food and money to these poor little mites.

Eventually, I managed to find a bridge over the main road and set off to find the park. The word park conjures up particular visions for me. Open green spaces and meandering paths lead to different aspects of the park. I was excited to see trees, shrubs, ponds, and wide-open spaces. Well, I was until I saw what was awaiting me. Now it's important to remember that this was the 1980s. Things may well have improved over the decades. If they had, sadly, I did not get to see it. My airline, British Airways, decided it was too dangerous for its crews to stay in central Nairobi. Instead, we moved to an airport hotel; such a shame.

And so eventually, I found myself in Uhuru Park. Unfortunately, it turned out to be more of an urban wasteland than a park. Litter, abandoned machinery, graffiti and goodness knows what else lay strewn across the landscape. There were groups of individuals hanging around, most of whom did not look like the friendly, welcoming locals I was hoping to meet. Not to be cheated out of my run, I decided to continue around the edge of the park. Venturing deeper inside, I had decided would be a little daft, not that careless choices had necessarily ever stopped me before. However, common sense, the least common of all the senses, prevailed, and I continued running around the fringes of the park. By this time, the heat and the thin air were beginning to have an effect on me. I noticed my breathing was becoming more laboured as I tried to fill my lungs with oxygen. The temperature was now in the mid-thirties, very high for a city six thousand feet above sea level. I had been running for thirty minutes, so I decided it was time to turn back. I also had a grumpy captain to face on the golf course. I dare not be late for that.

The return run took me, once again, through the streets of lost children. By the time I arrived back at the hotel, all other thoughts and plans had been erased. All I could think of was collecting money, returning to the streets, and giving as much help as I possibly could. The grumpy captain could find someone else to play golf with. Now, I had more important things to do. A brief conversation with the concierge desk changed all that.

I was informed that these children were orphans whose parents had died from a new and savage disease called HIV or AIDS! From that moment onwards, I was determined to do my best to help long-term in any way I could. I did go out again that afternoon with money and food. However, far more importantly, I started a twenty-year association with the Nyumbani Orphanage. This charity took these children off the streets and gave them a home. Because they had the deadly disease, none of them would live long enough to enjoy all of their teenage years. It was with a very heavy heart and a deep melancholy that I did indeed play golf with the grumpy captain.

As expected, I lost.

Chapter 11

The Rainbow Nation

Another city where running was not straightforward was Johannesburg in South Africa. When I first visited, apartheid was still very much alive and kicking. It was apparent in all of its hideous forms in all aspects of South African life.

Once again, I found myself in a hot and high city. Johannesburg is on the highveld at six thousand feet, similar to Nairobi. It was not then, and is still not, a safe place to run in. In forty years, I would have only set out to run through the streets of Johannesburg if I was being chased by someone who wanted my money. It would not be a case of if I would get mugged; it would be a case of when. It is a deeply troubled and dangerous place to be. That said, South Africa is still one of my favourite countries on the planet. It is a vibrant, exciting country where the majority of the people are friendly and welcoming. Sadly, it also has a dark and sinister underbelly, which is more prevalent in Johannesburg than in any other city I have visited in South Africa. So, over the decades, I have had to adapt my running to fit in with safety restrictions imposed on me. Most of the hotels our crews stayed in were based in Sandton, a relatively wealthy and safe enclave in the heart of the city.

We moved around various hotels several times over the years, and my running tracks adapted as we moved. One hotel, the Radisson Blu, apparently had the perfect setup, an indoor running track built around the inside of the hotel. I had heard rumours of this track, but I was genuinely amazed at what I found. There, on the tenth floor, was indeed, a running track that weaved itself around the entire circumference of the hotel. You entered and followed a winding trail with the occasional view of the outside world. Of course, I had become used to the running machines in hotel gyms, but this was a completely new experience. Obviously, the track was short; it took only about four minutes to complete a lap. As I ran for an hour, it did not take long before I became dizzy. To counter this, I turned around and started to run the other way around. Sadly, I soon found myself running into people. After a lot of shouting and swearing, not by me, my attention was drawn to the footprints painted on the track. So that was what they meant. I had thought it strange that the hotel thought it necessary to point out that your feet should be on the ground. They were there to tell me in which direction I should be running. Who would have thought?

Once the novelty of indoor running had literally run its course, I looked enviously out of one of the few windows along the track. I stopped in amazement when I saw a small park directly opposite the hotel. In the middle of the park was a giant tethered balloon which was being used to give joy rides to the tourists. That, however, was not what interested me. It was a track around the small park that held me spellbound. Unfortunately, I lingered too long at the window, and the runners I had run into a short while before now ran straight into me. A lot more shouting and swearing ensued. This time, however, I did not care; I had found an escape route. Never again was I to use that indoor track; after all that swearing and shouting, I thought I would be safer outside in the big balloon park. At least there, I could run either way and stop if I wanted to.

And so, onto one of my favourite running cities, indeed one of my favourite cities in the world. The incredible Mother City, Cape Town, where else?

I fell in love with Cape Town the moment I first flew over Table Mountain. I was flying the 747 manually, starting a gentle descending turn to the left over False Bay and lining up with the northern runway. Sheer scenic perfection combined with great air traffic controllers and an empty sky. What more could any pilot or any runner want?

When I first started flying to Cape Town, our hotel was far from the city. We were based near Somerset West, a nice hotel but isolated from the main attractions. I would set off on a run along the main road and then head off into the nearby housing estates. The runs were arduous because the terrain was undulating, some parts particularly steep. However, nowhere else near enough held any particular attraction for me. The area was relatively safe to run through, although this was still South Africa, so it paid to be on your guard at all times. Once away from the hotel complex, the area became more remote. I never carried any valuables, just enough cash to satisfy any would-be muggers, hopefully. Luckily for me, I never had to resort to bargaining for my life. Other tourists at the time were not so lucky. Then, we moved hotels to Sea Point.

This is a small town set on the coast between Cape Town and Camps Bay. It sits next to Clifton, where some of the most expensive properties in the world are located. For a runner, it is like having all your dreams and wishes come true at the same time. There were, basically, two types of runs that could be done from Sea Point. One run took you along the stunningly beautiful shoreline; the other took you up into the hills towards the base of Table Mountain, Lion's Head and the Twelve Apostles. What's not to like?

In all the years I ran in this area, I never had any cause to be concerned for my safety. There was a very remote trail along the base of the Twelve Apostles known as the pipe track. Not very imaginatively, it was named after the water pipe that the track followed. I ran the length of it without ever seeing another human being. Locals warned me not to become isolated; safety was in numbers. But there were times when you had to take risks, and to me, the incredible scenery justified any risk. The run would start from the hotel with a steep climb up to the Upper Kloof Road. When I say steep, I mean steep. Within minutes of setting off, my legs were burning, and my heart was pumping, and this was just the first few steps of an eighteen-kilometre run! Head down, arms pumping, there followed a gruelling climb as Kloof Road wound itself around the base of Lion's Head. Thirty minutes later, you turned left and started an even steeper climb as the road began its proper ascent. Usually, I took the Roundhouse Road, which offered a little breather as it descended towards a beautiful restaurant and outside bar. The view from here over Camps Bay was truly spectacular, especially at sunset with a cold beer or glass of wine in hand. That was only a distant dream as I started an even steeper climb back towards Kloof Road, the penalty for the earlier slight descent. It was a seemingly never-ending series of sharp, tight turns until eventually, you reached the crossroads with Camps Bay drive. Here, there was a choice of routes, all of which I tried at one time or another.

I turned towards Camps Bay. The views to my right were some of the most spectacular I had ever seen. The whole of Camps Bay was displayed in all of its glory. The wild Atlantic Ocean was crashing into the rocky coastline of Clifton. From my vantage point, I could make out the three small sandy beaches of Clifton and the vast expanse of the glorious Camps Bay beach.

Memories of my first attempt at swimming off this beach flooded back. Laying in the hot African sun, I thought it was time to cool off. I ran and dived into the waves. The shock was immediate and dramatic. I knew Great White sharks patrolled these shores, waiting for their next meal. The shock and pain as I hit the water were so intense that I thought I had shown up on their menu and they were not hanging around for starters. As my head surfaced and I struggled for breath, the next Atlantic roller hit me straight in the face. Down I went again. My whole body was in shock, and I struggled to breathe.

As I surfaced again, I realised I was not fighting a shark. I was fighting the intense cold of the water. On the beach, the temperature was in the mid-thirties. The south Atlantic sea temperature was barely above freezing. The sudden variation in temperatures had literally taken my breath away. I had never before swum in such freezing water. Think of swimming in the English Channel in January and then double the coldness of the water. That's how cold the seas were off the shores in Cape Town. It took me a while to understand why the water was so damn cold. It was when I realised that the next land mass after South Africa was Antarctica. I beat a hasty retreat from the water and spent the next few minutes trying to thaw out in the hot African sun.

Shuddering at the memory, I turned away from the views and concentrated once again on my run. The route now took me away from the ocean vista and towards the pipe track that followed the majestic line of the Twelve Apostles. I had been warned not to leave the relative safety of the road and follow this dirt track. Apparently, there had been attacks in the past. I had nothing on me except about twenty pounds in local currency to, hopefully, appease any would-be attacker. As I made my way along the track, immediately, I was rewarded with the spectacular vision of the cloud formation covering the tops of the Apostles. These layer-type clouds usually formed in the late afternoon when the wind came in from a south-westerly direction. The air mass had moved across the Atlantic Ocean and was heavily laden with moisture. As the air moved inland, it hit Table Mountain and the Twelve Apostles. With nowhere else to go, the air was forced onto the top of the mountain and was cooled rapidly. Unable to sustain the water, the clouds created the famous tablecloth that often sits atop the mountain. This cloud layer was then pushed over the mountainside and tumbled down towards Camps Bay and Cape Town. As it descended, it warmed up, and the cloud, or tablecloth, disappeared as quickly as it formed. This magical natural phenomenon was being played out in front of me as I made my way along the pipe track. I can think of nowhere else on the planet that mother nature played her games in such a dramatic fashion. It was simply mesmerising and stunning. Of course, running along a stony path and gazing up at the mountains can only have one outcome. Once again, I fell flat on my face.

Running and falling go hand in hand. Run, and eventually, you will trip over something, especially if you are off-road. I have often launched myself into space as a tree root, or boulder has grabbed one of my feet. Usually, I try to do a parachute roll as I make contact with the ground. This can work really well. I have even impressed myself at times as I fall, roll, and stand up, all in one seemingly effortless manoeuvre. Today sadly, was not one of those days. Instead of a spectacular recovery befitting a seasoned SAS operative, I went down like an express lift. Not only did I go straight down, somehow, I managed to do a half roll into a thorn bush, which immediately claimed me as if I was a long-lost relative. It had me in its thorny grasp and had no intention of letting go without a fight. The more I struggled, the more tenacious the bush became. As I lay there, feeling very sorry for myself, I remembered the warning signs along the track. This was a snake-infested area. And where do snakes like to spend their afternoons? Yep, I was in Mr

Snake's front room without an invite. Thoughts of prickles and thorns suddenly went straight down my list of priorities. I needed to vacate this bush and vacate it pretty damn quick.

A few painful moments later, I lay back on the path, staring at the clouds slowly rolling down the mountains. Their sheer beauty was, however, lost on me as I tried to assess the damage that had occurred over the last few problematic manoeuvres. Carefully, I tried to move each limb; luckily, they all seemed to be attached and moving when asked to. Sitting up, I looked down at my arms and legs. They had definitely not escaped uninjured. The thick, sharp thorns of the thorn bush had performed their roles admirably. I leaked blood from both legs and arms. The only good thing was that it looked worse than it was. Wiping away the red rivulets, I saw that the damage was mainly superficial. It was at that moment I noticed, to my horror, that something had sustained massive and permanent damage. I was mortified; how could I finish my run or return to civilisation in this state?

To be fully aware of the damage, I dragged myself to my feet and looked down at my front. The damage was even worse than I had first feared. In my haste to vacate myself from the vice-like grip of the thorn bush, I had left an essential part of me behind. I blinked and looked again, hoping that my eyes were deceiving me. Sadly not.

Hanging from one of the deadly branches were long threads of black material, which only moments ago had formed the majority of the front part of my running shorts. My gaze went from the bush back to what remained of my shorts. I could quite clearly see my man bits, luckily still where they should be and undamaged. If I could see them, then as soon as I got back on the road, so would everyone else. I still had over ten kilometres to go, most of which were along main roads. Worst of all, I had to run along the beachfront at Camps Bay, a place brimming with fast cars and beautiful people. This was going to be interesting, to say the least.

I tried taking the remnants of my shorts off and wearing them back to front. All this did was to expose my rear and running with back-to-front shorts is nigh on impossible. And so I did the only thing I could think of in these excruciatingly embarrassing circumstances; I ran while holding my running vest top in front of me. I tried tying it around my waist, but it soon moved sideways to expose what I was desperate to keep covered. No, the only way I could try to maintain some form of decency was to hold my vest in front of me to preserve a modicum of dignity.

This worked reasonably well until I approached the main promenade at Camps Bay. The seafront comprises a long line of trendy restaurants and bars. By now, it was late morning, and every pavement table was full of people enjoying an early lunch. The scene was one of very upmarket eateries populated by beautiful people flanked by expensive parked cars set against a stunning background.

And then, a filthy runner, legs smeared with blood, topless, and holding an equally filthy top in front of him runs past in front of this tranquil scene. It took me ten searingly and intensely embarrassing minutes to complete my run along the seafront. I could feel the faces of the customers turn and follow my progress. I was mortified as desperately, I tried to keep my running vest in the correct position. I still had another thirty minutes to go before I reached the hotel.

Eventually, I stumbled into the hotel leaving a trail of astonished guests in my wake as I queued up to get a replacement door key. My original key was still somewhere in that thorny bush. As I made my way into my room to tend to my wounds, I reflected that it was not one of my most enjoyable runs in Cape Town.

The other run I enjoyed immensely was the route along the shoreline to Cape Town itself. This was a more leisurely run as it followed a mainly flat path all the way to the Cape Town stadium, built for the 2010 FIFA World Cup. This route was a lot more popular than my mountain run. Whereas I never saw another runner on the mountain routes, I was never alone on this beachfront track. Runners were everywhere; all seemed to be running at a pace I had to work hard at to keep up with. I have always hated being overtaken. Even if the person attempting to pass me was thirty years my junior, I could not help myself. I had to accelerate or attempt to accelerate to stay ahead. It took me a long time to realise that many of the runners I valiantly tried to outpace were on a much shorter run than I was attempting. A ten-minute race would leave them at the end of their workout whilst I still had another five or ten kilometres to go. Despite realising this, I still strived to avoid being overtaken. It's been one of my many faults. Although this run lacked the dramatic scenery of the pipe track, it still offered treats that few other runs can hope to match.

I would set off from the hotel, and instead of turning right up the hill, I would turn left and follow the road into a gentle descent to the beach road. With the Atlantic waves crashing against the rocks to my left, I would head towards the enormous outdoor swimming pool set directly on the shoreline. As the sea was icy cold, this pool provided locals and visitors alike with the only opportunity to enjoy a swim without freezing to death or becoming a shark's lunch. On scorching days, the queues would stretch along the promenade an hour before the pool even opened.

Passing this attraction, I would continue to follow the promenade towards Greenpoint. With Table Mountain coming into view on my right, along with the Lion's Head and Signal Hill, the contrast to the ocean was complete. Often, I would watch as paragliders were launched from Lion's Head. These huge canopies, generally with two people hanging below them, would make their winding way down through a series of lazy and sharp turns to land on the grassy area literally yards away from where I was running.

From here, my run took me inland towards the huge Cape Town stadium, around it and through the beautiful Greenpoint Park. This park runs alongside the golf course and is interspersed with lakes and picnic areas. Pushing on, the route took me back towards the seafront, a turn to the left along the sea wall, following the promenade back towards Seapoint and the hotel. A few times during a run, a sea fret would suddenly move onshore, and everything would be covered in a white mist. Visibility, which moments earlier had been unlimited, would be reduced to just a few feet. At this point, the eerie siren of Greenpoint Lighthouse would sound to warn shipping of the hidden danger in the outcrop of rocks just off the shoreline. Then, as suddenly as it had appeared, the fog would retreat, once again allowing the sun to glint off the dramatic scenery - simply stunning and something I have only ever experienced on this run. By the time I passed the swimming pool again, I had completed fifteen kilometres. From here, I would continue past the hotel and run into Clifton. This section of the run involved the only steep incline as the road took me up onto the main road back into Sea Point. When eventually, I reached the hotel, I would be a mixture of sweat and huge, satisfied smiles. The other good thing about this run was that I always managed to return safely without injury and with my dignity intact.

Chapter 12

The Dark Side

Whilst the Mother City was my favourite African run, Lagos was most certainly my least favourite.

Whereas Cape Town and Johannesburg were five-day trips, Lagos, with a flight time of six hours, was only a night stop. With such a short layover, I was always happy to run around the hotel grounds and tennis courts. Ten laps were around five kilometres. Although it was a boring run, it made for an excellent warm-up before visiting the gym. This hotel gym was a relatively new addition. It is memorable for an incident when I resorted to using the running machine as the rain poured down outside. It was far too wet to run around the hotel. I was pounding away on the dreaded conveyor belts when the gym was suddenly hit by a deafening blast of thunder and lightning. This was far too exciting for the corrugated iron roof, which got up and left the building. I was quite sad to see it go as it left me on an electrical machine in the middle of a thunderstorm. Thankfully, the belt was made of rubber which protected me as sparks flew around the gym while the electrical circuits protested at this new onslaught of water. I should have run outside, after all. I would have stayed drier and safer.

On another memorable flight down to Lagos, my colleague asked me what I intended to do once we had landed. I gave my usual answer of a few beers that night and my regular routine of running, going to the gym and swimming. He then enquired what I would do with the other three days?

I had been called out on standby for this flight. The phone had rung at home, and within ten minutes, I was racing towards the airport. The crew controller had failed to inform me that this trip was six days instead of the usual three-day one. No wonder the original captain had gone sick. I was now faced with three whole days in a place I really did not want to be in.

The first day went according to plan, lots of laps of the hotel grounds, followed by a bit of gym and a swim. I repeated the process on day two, but by the third day, I was thinking of digging a tunnel and making my escape. Instead, I looked at Google maps and planned a run around the local area. In retrospect, I should have stayed with the tunnel plan. It would have been safer.

By the following day, I had my route all planned out, and I was ready to run. Lagos is a dangerous place, and I was under no illusions that I had to take precautions. Instead of taking my phone, I decided to draw my route out on a piece of hotel notepaper. I also took off my Apple watch. I do not wear any jewellery, so I was now a poor target for any would-be muggers. Of course, I had my twenty-dollar appeasement note tucked safely away in one of my socks. With the preparations complete, I made my way downstairs.

The hotel was set in its own extensive grounds, and when I first flew to Lagos in 1988, it was the only half-decent hotel in

Lagos. Over the decades, other more modern hotels have sprung up. However, we remained in the now dated hotel I had first stayed in. The hotel was set on its own grounds and was heavily fortified. Departing from this compound, you were out into the vast and chaotic Lagos suburbs. I ran up to the guard post and waited for them to lift the barriers to allow me to pass. The barriers remained firmly closed. 'I may have to dig that tunnel after all', I thought.

Lagos has never been regarded as the most secure place on the planet. From my first to my last visit, the arrival and departure routine has always been the same. We would be met by armed guards on landing and escorted through immigration and customs. They would then lead us to two waiting buses, one for the crew and one for the luggage. When I say armed, I mean a fully armed escort. We would all crowd onto our bus, followed by three soldiers. All the curtains on the bus had to be drawn shut to prevent onlookers from knowing who was on board. Then, we would be given a safety lecture by the self-proclaimed bus captain.

In full military style uniform, we were informed that if we were attacked, we should hide under the seats. At the same time, the guards would shoot as many of the attackers as possible. The four guards from the luggage bus would also join in and help to protect us. This luggage bus drove in front of us and blocked the roads to allow us safe passage when turning. If all of this was meant to shock us into the reality of life in Lagos, it certainly did the trick for some of our younger and less experienced cabin crew. On quite a few occasions, I noticed the bottom lip of the first timers to Lagos start to tremble, as I'm sure mine had done on more than a few occasions.

Standing by the guards' hut, requesting access to the outside world four decades later, it seemed my survival instincts had been dulled. Nothing serious had ever happened on any of the bus journeys, and stupidly, I assumed that the precautions taken were overly cautious. Two guards left their fortified position to approach this mad guest attempting to leave the compound's safety. I started to explain my plan to them, and the look of shock on their faces should have been enough for me to apologise for being such an idiot. I should have humbly turned around and run around the tennis courts. Sadly I didn't do that. 'This was India all over again', I thought to myself.

Whilst one of the guards examined my planned route, the other kept a close eye on anyone passing by on the pavement. His hand was always on the rifle at his side. This was another clue I missed which should have informed me that my plan was plain dumb. After five minutes of trying to dissuade me, eventually, the guards had to let me go. This was, after all, a hotel, not a prison. And so off I ran, map in hand, looking forward to seeing the real Lagos, not just a hotel compound. In retrospect, I was hugely lucky that this did not turn out to be my last ever run, or indeed my last ever anything. This idiot abroad disappeared into the maze of roads that made up this part of the greater Lagos area. It would have been my fault if I had never been seen again, and I accepted later that due to my hubris, I deserved everything that came my way.

These, however, were not the thoughts in my mind as I left the main road to follow my pre-planned route. For the first ten minutes, all went well. The road names that I had carefully written down came up as expected. I began to relax and disregard some of the apprehension the guards had sown in my very small brain. It was a sweltering and humid day, and I noticed that large and menacing thunderstorms were beginning to form. This is not unusual in Lagos. I calculated that I would be back at the hotel before the storm arrived, another misjudgement.

My next turning point came and went as expected. I was starting to enjoy myself. I was even being joined by some young children; 'how cute', I thought to myself. But these children were so excited to see this foreigner that they started to throw small stones to help me on my way. Not so cute. Maybe, this was a local tradition to welcome strangers, and so on I ran, with only a few minor stings where the stones had, inadvertently, hit me.

As I continued on my way, I began to notice that the children were now getting bigger and the objects thrown my way were getting larger. A few found their painful mark, and I began to accelerate and duck, simultaneously trying to get away from this small but growing mob that was now pursuing me. I was still clinging to the hope that this was just some young teenagers having a bit of what they considered fun. And then, I saw what was awaiting me at the end of the road I was running along. To my horror, a group of young men was brandishing various evil-looking implements. These were designed to seriously damage whoever was unlucky enough to be on the receiving end of their use.

Real fear now gripped me. I was in severe and dire trouble. I did what any sensible person would do. I turned and fled as fast as I could. Sadly for me, this was not a great plan. I had disregarded the fact that I was being pursued by a growing collection of youngsters. 'At least I could run through this crowd', I thought to myself. I had yet to lose an argument with an eleven-year-old. Frighteningly for me, they had all now been joined by their much bigger brothers. I stopped dead. I looked behind me, and the young men slowly advanced towards me with their weapons held menacingly in front of them. The crowd, now in front of me, started to advance slowly. I was furious, not scared, just bloody furious at my own stupidity and furious that these people would inflict serious, if not fatal, damage on me. I had done nothing more than run, or attempted to run, through their streets.

It is almost impossible to predict how you are going to react when put in a position of extreme danger. Thankfully, I had never before felt that my life was under immediate threat. I knew in a moment of absolute clarity that I would be very fortunate ever to see my family again. It was that single thought that made me react in the way I did. How dare these people think they had a right to deprive my family and me of a future together. I seized one of the sticks that had been thrown at me and raised it above my head. Whoever would be the first to attack me was going down, as were the next few before the inevitable happened. I stood my ground. The adrenaline coursed through me. My fight-or-flight response had well and truly kicked in. I had no choice but to fight. I swore loudly at my attackers as I awaited my fate. I remember hoping my life insurance policy was in order, making me laugh and swear simultaneously. My attackers must have thought they had come across a madman.

Now, I would like to say that after fending off the first few attackers, the rest were so frightened that they turned and fled. They did, in fact, turn and ran away, but it was nothing to do with me. As I stood there bracing myself for the onslaught, I heard loud horns blasting from what sounded like a convoy of trucks. Everyone turned to look to see what was happening. From around the corner, two large open-air Toyota land cruisers screeched to a stop just yards from where I stood. People were having to jump sideways to avoid being run over. Six heavily armed guards jumped out of the trucks and began swinging large truncheons as they began to disperse the crowd to get to me. I noticed that armed guards also stood in the trucks with their rifles raised, ready to shoot. 'This could go one of two ways', I thought to myself, as I was seized by the guards and dragged towards one of the trucks,

I was thrown unceremoniously into the back of the truck as the guards continued to swing their truncheons indiscriminately at anyone who was stupid enough to get within striking distance. I lay in the bottom of the truck as we sped away, hopefully, towards the safety of the hotel compound.

A few minutes later, I stood in front of the hotel, a very chastened, subdued and apologetic man. Not only had I selfishly ignored the guards' advice, but I had also put them in great danger with my stupid actions. If I had not shown the guards my planned route, they would never have found me, and I have no doubt that I would not be here today and able to write about my rescue.

I asked the guards to give me five minutes. I ran off again, and I could see the consternation and trepidation on their faces. This time though, I was off to my room. I always carried two hundred American dollars with me just for any unforeseen eventualities. Grabbing the money, I returned to where the guards were waiting. I shared out the dollars and was glad to see they were happy to receive this very small token of my gratitude. Two hundred dollars is a small price to pay for saving your life.

I never ran in Lagos again. I knew that I had undoubtedly used all my nine lives in one short run. From then on, I also paid close attention to the bus captain's safety briefings every time I visited the city.

Things were so different just down the road in Accra, the capital of Ghana. Although it was only a few hundred miles from Lagos, it was like being on a different planet. Happily, I set off from the hotel, iPhone in my pocket and Apple Watch on my wrist. Although Accra is a large, noisy, crowded city, I ran along the roads and suburbs without fear of being accosted or chased. Indeed, the opposite occurred; people seemed slightly surprised to see me running but smiled and waved anyway. How strange that two geographically close cities can differ so widely in their society and culture.

Another city where I had a not-so-warm welcome, was Marrakesh, Morocco. Liz and I were on holiday and staying just outside the Medina, the enormous old walled city. This pink-walled city is vast and consists of a labyrinth of small dark alleyways containing thousands of small markets and shops. Set foot inside, and you are immediately accosted by hundreds of vendors and beggars trying to relieve you of your last penny. You are literally, pulled and pushed from one to the other. You have to be very insistent in declining their attention before they move on to their next victim. On our very first day, we were out walking in the Medina. Stupidly, we were naive enough to ask a local for directions back to the main square. Our self-appointed guide instructed us to follow him, something I was very hesitant to do. As we were led deeper into the dark and increasingly sinister alleyways, I noticed that there were no other tourists in this part of the Medina.

Suddenly, our guide turned and demanded money, a lot of money. I tried to explain that once we were back in the main square, I would change some notes and pay him for his time and trouble. Apparently, this was not acceptable to him, and he lunged at me and attempted to take the money I had in my pockets. He also made a grab for my watch and phone.

This was not good news. We were deep in the maze, and I was with my wife. We were highly vulnerable, and our attacker probably carried some sort of weapon. Also, I guessed that he had brought us here, where he had friends and backup.

If you are alone, it is much easier to be reckless and attempt to fight or flee. The flight options quickly disappear when you have your wife at your side. I had to fight and fight quickly before our assailant's friends made an appearance. As my attacker made his move, I grabbed him none too gently by the throat and lifted him back against the wall behind us. Then, I tapped his head delicately against the wall a couple of times to improve his manners and remind him not to mug tourists. After this quick lesson, I let him slowly crumple to the ground. Remembering that he was probably armed, I stood heavily on the side of his knee to be sure that he could not follow us. I didn't know that knees could talk, but the noise from his joint did sound very much like a scream. Even I winced!

Of course, I had completely forgotten about the possibility of more assailants. The flight option quickly became the best bet. Grabbing my wife's hand, we ran into the first shop we came across. Luckily, the owner spoke good English and seemed a jolly decent type. Once we explained our predicament, kindly, he showed us to a rear door through which we fled. Despite being in Marrakech for another five days, we never dared return to the Medina. I was sure there was a knife with my name on it lurking in some dark corner.

However, of course, I decided to go running away from the Medina. What more could possibly go wrong? Setting off from the hotel, I had what I considered to be an excellent and hopefully, safe route marked out and the run itself went very much as planned. What I was not prepared for was the reaction of the locals. I was sworn and spat at by a significant number of the people I ran past. I was running well away from the tourist areas, and all I could think of was that I had upset them by wearing shorts and a vest. I never found out as I spent the remainder of my time in Marrakech locked safely away in the hotel's beautiful grounds. Sometimes, you have to accept that gyms and running machines are the safest options in some countries.

Running in Africa was never dull. The continent holds so much variety and diversity. Running through the most incredible scenery and some of the most deprived areas on earth, you always have to be on your guard, ready to be amazed or terrified. Nowhere else on earth can match this magnificent continent, but if you go running there, be prepared for the unexpected.

I had managed to come out of this encounter as somewhat of a hero to my wife. Our next adventure in Africa had a very different outcome.

Chapter 13

Getting Up to Monkey Business

The idea of visiting the mysterious and exotic island of Zanzibar had always held a fascination for me. Unfortunately, the route to Daar es Salaam, the closest major international airport, was operated by a Boeing 767, not the 747 that I flew. Therefore, there was no other choice but to take a holiday to the island rather than visit it on a working trip. The fact that Freddie Mercury of Queen fame grew up on the island only added to the allure. The decision was made and we set off for another adventure, one that nearly cost me my life.

After the long flight down to the east coast of Africa, Liz and I found ourselves onboard a little twin-engined aircraft for the relatively short flight from Daar es Salaam to the paradise that is Zanzibar. The plane was a ten-seater, high-winged Twin Otter. I was lucky enough to sit in the co-pilot's seat. There was only one pilot, and all the other seats were occupied. I watched how the pilot had to do everything from loading the passengers and their baggage to organising the fuel and flight plan. I was transported right back to my early flying days. Immediately, I related to everything she was doing and offered to help, but sensibly, she refused.

On the flight over to Zanzibar, which lasted about fifty minutes, I asked her about flying in these parts of the world and if she intended to stay here or move onto the airlines. Again, I was met with a quizzical stare. Obviously, she regretted having chosen me to sit next to her. When I asked if I could have a go at the landing, finally, she lost her calm demeanour and asked who the bloody hell I was? I had actually only been joking about the landing; it had been many years since I had landed a Twin Otter, and then it was on water, not land. I explained that I was also a pilot and had started my career doing a similar job to the one she was now doing.

We had a very interesting conversation lasting for the remainder of the flight. After we had landed, I left her the name and contact details of the recruitment department of British Airways. Wishing her luck in her career, I hoped she no longer regretted having chosen me to sit next to her.

Zanzibar is everything I expected it to be, wild, untamed and utterly beautiful. Flying here twice a day was much better than sitting for up to sixteen hours in an airliner. I hoped our pilot made the decision that was right for her.

Initially, we stayed on the island's east coast, not the best side, as we soon discovered. The coastline was rocky, and beaches were scarce. A quick hop in a taxi and a tour of the hotels on the west coast ended with us standing in the reception area of an all-inclusive Italian resort hotel. The whole place was a sheer luxury; best of all, it was situated on one of the most beautiful beaches I had ever seen. This place was obviously going to be way out of our price range. Still, nothing ventured, nothing gained, as they say. Tentatively, I enquired if they had a room available for the next week.

The receptionist explained in broken English that this was an all-inclusive resort and could only be booked on the internet or through a travel company. Well, that seemed to be that, and as we turned to leave, I had a brainwave. Turning back to the receptionist, I asked if I could speak to the manager. When he arrived, I showed him my airline pass and enquired if they gave any discounts to the travel industry. I explained that we had stayed at a hotel on the east coast and would not be giving it a very good review. We can report back with a favourable review if we stay at his resort. He did not enquire why a pilot would be writing hotel reviews. Luckily, I had hidden the pilot bit of my identity card with a large thumb.

For a remarkably good price, we found ourselves in a beautiful suite. We had everything we could possibly want. Even the towels on the bed had been made to look like two swans embracing. Red rose petals sprinkled over the bed completed the effect. I tried to emulate the romantic ambience when we got home. Sadly, it looked more like two towels had gotten into a fight to the death with blood liberally splashed around. I substituted geranium petals without going to the expense of rose petals. Not only did they not have the desired effect, they stained the sheets permanently. Best leave this sort of thing to the experts in the tropics, I decided, after a severe telling-off. Anyway, at this point, I was in my wife Liz's very good books. Unsurprisingly, this state of affairs only lasted for a very short period of time.

We were lying on the beach later that day, watching the waves lap gently against the golden sand. Scattered along this seemingly endless beach, there were about twenty wooden fishing vessels, known locally as Ngalawa boats. They were basically hollowed-out tree trunks with an outrigger on either side to provide stability. They were still being used here on a daily basis. They must have got the design right, as nothing had changed over the centuries. Patrolling the shores were tall and graceful figures dressed in traditional African robes. Although they looked magnificent, these were warriors, and their long and deadly knives were certainly not there for ceremonial purposes. No, these were Maasai warriors, from southern Kenya and the north of Tasmania.

They were employed by the hotels in Zanzibar, not for their striking appearance but for their fierce fighting reputation. If you decide to break into a hotel protected by these men, you had better have a good escape plan.

There we were, lying on an idyllic beach, fishermen lazing in their boats and Maasai warriors patrolling the grounds. This should have been enough for anyone to settle down, read a book, order a drink, or … you guessed it, plan a run.

At the time, smartphones were still science fiction. Although I owned a mobile phone, it only did what it said on the packet, it made telephone calls, end of.

Looking along the shoreline, I noticed another beautiful, vast expanse of sand just over the headland. Undoubtedly, there would be another colossal beach just beyond that one. A plan had hatched in a not-too-large brain. As I was not too fond of a there-and-back run, always preferring a circular route, I planned to run along the road from the hotel until I found an access point leading to the beach. From there, I would run along the coastline until I returned from where I had started. What could be simpler?

Despite her loudly voiced concerns ringing in my ears, I left Liz to enjoy the remains of the afternoon sun and asked her to keep an eye out for me as I ran back along the beach.

I set off along a newly tarmacked road on a hot, scorching afternoon. I decided to run for thirty minutes before attempting to find my way to the beach for the return run back to the hotel. All went very well for the first thirty minutes. It was only after I left the road in an attempt to find the coastline that things went rapidly downhill. I began looking for roads or tracks leading to the coast. From looking at a map, I knew that the road ran parallel to the shore; a short distance to my right, an azure blue sea awaited me. Once I reached the beach, turning right and heading back to the hotel would be simple. The theory was fine; the reality, of course, was a little more complicated.

A track suddenly appeared as I rounded a corner. I was hoping for something a little more prominent but it seemed to fit the bill. Initially, it appeared to offer a way to the beach. And so, rather stupidly, I set off down this unmarked path. Although I had no smartphone, I owned one of the very new and expensive Apple iPods. It was my pride and joy, and I had downloaded nearly fifty running tunes to help me on my way. This rather large and bulky item was kept in a pouch around my waist with wires attached to the small white earbuds.

Suddenly, the track became very narrow, and I found myself scrambling over rocks and shrubs in an effort to find the coast. This should have served as a warning not to go any further. It would have been much more sensible to turn around and find a proper road. Instead, I could now hear the waves lapping against the shore and so I continued on my way, seduced by the sound of the water. My plan literally appeared to be back on track. How wrong could I possibly be?

I broke through the undergrowth to find myself in a small, deserted cove. It was utterly beautiful, although not quite what I was expecting. Where was the vast expanse of golden sand that would lead me back to my sunbed and a cold beer? Undaunted, I turned right and ran towards the headland. Surely, after I climbed over that, the actual beach would reveal itself, but sadly not. As I rounded the point, I found myself in another almost identical cove with another rocky headland at the far side of the beach. This continued for some time, running along a small beach and climbing over rocks to be confronted with another small cove.

To my alarm, I began to realise that the further I ran, the higher the rocks in front and to the side of me were. Also, the sand on the beaches I ran along kept getting narrower. 'What the hell was going on?' I thought to myself, 'how can a beach disappear?' And then, I remembered that the tides in Zanzibar were notorious for their severity and speed. My goodness, I realised, that is precisely what was happening. The waves were coming in at a rate I had never seen before. The whole ocean appeared to be moving towards me. It was definitely time to get out of here. I reached the next headland only a few yards in front of me and peered over the rocks. There was no beach. It had been swallowed up by the approaching waves. There was nothing for it. I would have to turn around and follow my footsteps back to the path I had run down.

Sadly, however, there were no footprints in the sand behind me. In fact, there was no sand at all, the tide had seen to that. Despite this, I started back the way I had come. The sandy beaches were fast being swallowed up by the approaching ocean. One minute I was splashing in two inches of water; the next, I was wading waist-deep in the ocean. I held my precious iPod high above my head as I attempted to reach the next headland. At that precise moment, I had to accept the inevitable. My iPod was preventing me from swimming to safety. My music machine was history, and so would I be if I didn't do something drastic and do it very soon. As the mountain of water pulled me relentlessly towards sharp and jagged rocks, I let go of my iPod and my fifty carefully recorded songs. I swam desperately towards the shoreline or what was left of it. I clung onto the rocky base of a steep cliff as the waves began to intensify their pounding. There was only one way to go: directly up a thirty-foot vertical ridge. If I tried to swim or cling to the cliff, all would be lost, and I would almost certainly drown. That didn't inspire me, so I began the ascent.

I wouldn't say I like rock climbing, I never have and never will. I could not see the point of climbing a steep cliff face when you could stroll up the gentle incline on the other side. My hatred of this sport intensified as I turned away from the waves below. I knew my strength was being tested to the limit, and if I slipped back into the breaking waves, I would not have the strength to pull myself out again. 'This was just about as serious as it gets', I thought to myself, as I desperately clung onto the rock face for dear life.

Finally, after much swearing and many cuts and scrapes, I pulled myself up and over the top of the cliff. I rolled over onto my back and tried to regain my breath and get my heart rate back to something approaching normality. Pulling myself to my feet, I looked down at my front. To say I was a mess was an understatement. The rocks had been brutal on my clothes and skin. Both were in tatters. My beloved iPod lay somewhere on the ocean bed. At least it knew where it was, which was more than could be said for me.

I looked around feeling totally helpless. I was on a small ledge with the ocean to one side and the deep jungle on the other. The sun was starting to beat its hasty, but beautiful retreat below the horizon. To make matters even more interesting, there are no prolonged sunsets at these latitudes; one moment it's light, and thirty minutes later, it's dark. I reckoned I had about twenty of those thirty minutes of daylight left.

Time to move. Being trapped in a jungle at night was only slightly less appealing than fighting the waves I had left behind. The first problem was getting through the undergrowth. There were no paths, and I had nothing to help me beat a way through the sharp and thorny bushes. With a lot of cursing from the painful cuts being continually inflicted, I finally managed to find a small clearing. I was about at the end of my endurance. I sank to my knees in despair. Incredibly, despite being in a tropical jungle, I was cold, really cold. I was shivering. The adrenaline that had brought me this far had finally run out. With it, so had my chances of getting out of this dreadful place. The light was fading fast. I had only minutes before all around me would be plunged into darkness. Across the clearing, I could make out a small path, and like a moth to a flame, I pulled myself wearily to my feet and started to make my way towards it.

Without warning, I heard a terrible scream. Suddenly, a large and angry figure burst out of the foliage running straight towards me. Now, I usually would have been terrified, literally scared to death by the aggression of this creature. Normally, I would have turned and fled. Today, this apparition had picked on the wrong person to attack. Instead of being scared, I was furious. How dare this creature do this to me after the day I had endured. I turned on it, screamed back, and ran at it. In the gloom, I could now make out that my adversary was a very large, and very angry monkey.

Well, Mr Monkey was probably just showing off to his troupe and was caught entirely off guard by my sudden onslaught. The look of surprise on his face said it all as this madman returned his attack. Sensibly, he was the one that turned and fled. Never cross a wet, bloody and lost runner, I shouted after him. With this new adrenaline rush pumping through my veins, I made my way down this new track.

Darkness had now enveloped me, and each step was a step into the unknown. A jungle at night is not a good place to be alone, especially if you know that there are lots of nasty things just waiting to bite, scratch, or poison you. A little moonlight enabled me to break into a gentle jog as the pathway widened into a stony path which eventually led me onto the road I had run along on what seemed an eternity ago.

It took me another thirty minutes to return to where I had set off some two or three hours previously. I had lost all sense of time. I drew some inquisitive glances from the elegantly dressed Italians making their way into the restaurants. The manager I had spoken to that morning looked extremely crestfallen that he had allowed a mad Englishman into his beautiful hotel. If I thought the manager's reaction was a little extreme, I was about to wish I was back facing my monkey friend shortly after I knocked on my room door.

The only time I had ever seen Liz as angry as this was when, inadvertently, I sent a hundred years' worth of dust and rubble down a chimney and into our kitchen. Liz had been standing by the fireplace in her stewardess uniform when she was hit by this black cloud of debris. She stormed out of the back door, calling me names, some of which I hadn't heard before. Looking down from the roof, I could only see a debris-covered figure. Only her eyes were showing through the liberal covering of soot. I stayed on the roof until she had showered, changed, and gone to work.

Unfortunately for me, on this occasion, she was not going to work, so I got both barrels simultaneously. She had waited for my promised return on the beach until dusk fell. Frantic with worry, she had alerted the Maasai warriors, who had pledged to keep an eye out for me. She was about to call the police when I knocked on the door. I spent the rest of the evening trying to appease and apologise to her. I even tried to remake the swan towels she had thrown at me, but nothing worked. I could hardly blame her. That was my last run in Zanzibar. It should have been my last run, full stop. But, of course, it wasn't. There were plenty more running adventures to come.

Chapter 14

Six Green Bottles

We flew to many countries in the Middle East. Some I loved; others not so much, and one or two I have no desire ever to return to. Each country has a unique feel and a different attitude to runners on their streets.

Bahrain was always one of the places I was pleased to see on my roster. It was a relatively short flight, and the locals were always welcoming. We stayed in the capital, Manama, a small city that always looked half-finished. I would set off and run through the usually deserted streets until I reached the waterfront. From here, I would run along the promenade until I reached the marina. Despite its obvious wealth, Bahrain has never been overdeveloped, as have countries such as Dubai. Even so, the boats moored along the quay and marina were worth many times the price of my house. Instead of the opulent and flashy wealth favoured by its close neighbours, Bahrain somehow retained some of its original dignity.

After passing the marina, I would then cut back into the city and eventually, return to the hotel. The roads were only half finished, and care had to be taken to avoid ending up in one of the many potholes. On every corner, there seemed to be a new building under construction. Still, they were not the super skyscrapers that were being constructed elsewhere in the Middle Eastern countries. Bahrain respected its past, and despite recent political unrest, it always seemed to me to be one of the more stable countries in the region. The fact that alcohol was available in the hotel bars had nothing to do with my affection for the country.

All this was in great contrast to Dubai. When I first visited, I really liked the place. We stayed in a reasonably good hotel right on the waterfront. Our hotel was one of just a few hotels dotted along the creek. I would come out of the hotel and set off along the waterway. The sight, smells, and sounds of old Dubai were intoxicating. Ancient wooden Dhow fishing vessels were crowded together, each disgorging that day's catch. The ones not used for fishing were used as ferries to take people across the creek. The closest thing to a high-rise building was the very few hotels along the creek, but none were more than six stories high. Our hotel had no fridges in the rooms, we unscrewed the front grills of the air conditioning ducts and placed our beers there to keep them cold. Well, when I say we, I meant the smarter crews did that. Personally, I just drank warm beer.

My runs in those days were enjoyable, tranquil and relaxing, well apart from the brutal heat in the summer. Everything was super cheap. A beer cost less than a quarter of the price we paid at home. To make up for that, we drank four times as many beers, which seemed to even things up nicely. On my last visit to Dubai, I paid sixty pounds for four small bottles!

One of the first times I suffered the effects of heat exhaustion was in Dubai. This was in the 1980s when Dubai was a very different place. I set off for my early morning run. I knew that the summer temperatures would make running impossible later in the day, so I set off just as the sun rose. The temperature was in the high twenties but still bearable as I began to run along the creek into the breaking dawn. Unfortunately, or maybe luckily, there was no apparent circular route. I was planning to run for thirty minutes one way, then turn around and retrace my steps back to the hotel. And with that plan in mind, I began at a brisk pace; my first mistake. All went well for the first twenty minutes. There was a light breeze wafting in from the creek, and all seemed well with the world. The sights and sounds of old Dubai were intoxicating and kept me occupied. I was giving little thought to what I was attempting. I checked my watch and saw I had another ten minutes before I would turn around and head back. I was beginning to notice that the temperature had climbed a few degrees since sunrise. Still, it was a dry heat, and as yet, I had not even begun to sweat, so I pressed on. It was not time to turn back quite yet.

Ten minutes later and I was beginning to struggle. Although I was still sweat free, my legs were starting to feel like lead, an unusual feeling, even on the longest of my runs. At least now, I had turned around and was on my way back. I told myself only thirty minutes to go. Unfortunately, my arms had now joined my legs, beginning to feel twice their normal weight.

To distract myself from these uncomfortably new sensations, I tried to concentrate on watching the Dhows as they glided across the creek. As hard as I tried, I could not focus on a single boat; they all started to merge into one very large ship. To make matters even worse, this mirage of vessels then seemed to be floating, not on the water but about ten feet above it. I shook my head, which was a big mistake as my neck and shoulders were now struggling to support its weight. I felt for a moment they would fail, and my head would roll onto the pavement. That would mean I would have to carry it back with me, an added task I was not too keen to undertake.

At last, I could make out the distant outline of my hotel; not long to go now, thank goodness. Ten minutes later, the hotel was still as far away as it had been when I first noticed it. Surely, hotels can't move away from me at the same pace I could run towards them? My thought process had become somewhat deranged. What was wrong with me?

The sun was now high in the sky, and I appeared to be the only person still left on the creek. 'Where has everyone gone?' I thought to myself as I checked that my head was still attached and that the Dhows were still flying above the water. I still needed help to fathom why the hotel refused to appear any closer despite my best efforts to catch it. I decided to stop running while searching my brain for answers to sort out these little ambiguities. It was only then, when I looked down at my legs, I realised that they had stopped running a while ago. It was only my arms and brain that were still running. The rest of my body had obviously given up some time ago. Sure enough, I was running on the spot. I had not moved an inch in the last five minutes. At the time, I had no idea I was suffering from sunstroke and dehydration, a deadly combination. Holding onto a nearby bench, I tried to steady myself. The world was starting to revolve slowly, and my vision was becoming blurred and dim.

After a few minutes of rest, I felt a little better, well enough to attempt the walk back towards the hotel. The temperature rose with every passing minute, and I knew I had to get into the shade as quickly as possible. There were no buildings or shelters between me and the hotel. I had to press on or pass out. Every step was excruciatingly painful as my head felt like it would explode at any moment; the rest of my body was not far behind on the pain scale.

After what seemed an eternity, finally, I managed to stagger into the hotel's foyer. There were some very strange glances cast my way as I leaned against the wall in the hotel lobby, trying to get my eyes to focus and my head to stop pounding. Initially, the cool air of the lobby seemed to make matters worse, and I collapsed into an armchair, totally disoriented and feeling incredibly sick. I am still unsure how long I sat there before I could summon the energy to stand up and walk towards the lifts. Then, I noticed a large digital temperature display by the revolving entrance door. Squinting to bring the numbers into focus, I was only slightly surprised when I worked out that they read fifty-three degrees centigrade. 'Well, that would explain a lot', I thought to myself, as I sought out the blessed sanctuary of my room. I did not re-emerge until it was time to fly home later that night.

When I go running now in Dubai, instead of the beautiful Dhow boats of old, I run alongside a never-ending traffic jam. I come back coughing out car exhaust fumes and wishing things were different, or at least not as different as they now are. I am not a fan of the new Dubai, and I cannot see myself ever returning there.

Qatar sadly, also joins my list of places I have no desire to ever run in or visit again. I have never been a regular visitor to Doha; the aircraft I flew only occasionally went there. The main problem I had with this country was the lack of respect the Qataris showed to the vast number of poorly paid immigrant workers. They had brought them in to build their city, particularly the new football stadiums for the football World Cup. Yet they treated them with disdain and disrespect.

Exiting from the hotel was more like running into a giant building site. In other words, it was not exactly fun. On one occasion, we were escorted by our local agent through the airport for our flight home. One of these poor migrant had collapsed on the floor and had been knocked unconscious by the impact to his head. There was blood everywhere. Unbelievably, people were stepping around and over him. When we stopped to help, our agent tried to move us on. He didn't want any delay in our departure. When he tried to move me away as I bent down to help, the look I gave him persuaded him that if he didn't let go of me, he would soon be joining this unfortunate man. Our demands for medical assistance went unanswered right up to the point where I refused to fly home until help arrived. We waited there until the paramedics arrived. We left on time, and I felt that the best view of Qatar was from the flight deck window as we climbed into the night sky.

These countries all had their problems, or maybe it was actually me that had the issues. However, they were paradises compared to Saudi Arabia, and this time, it was definitely not me who had the problem.

I always respected the country I visited and always obeyed the local laws and traditions. I was a visitor in their country and regarded it as my duty, and that of our flight crew, to respect that country. I didn't mind that we were not allowed to drink in Saudi Arabia. In fact, I always thought of it as an excellent excuse to give my liver a rest. Some old-school flight engineers used to empty their mouthwash bottles and replace the contents with vodka and a green dye. When they informed me of this trick, I asked not to know. If they wanted to risk imprisonment for a drink, that was up to them. I could certainly live without alcohol for a few days.

What I found very difficult to live with, however, was how our female crew members were treated. A local ground crew assistant once refused to accept a fuel order from our female co-pilot. On another occasion, we were waiting for our hotel lift door to open. Suddenly, a Saudi man walked up to our senior cabin crew member and spat in her face. Apparently, he disapproved of females standing in front of men in the queue. Luckily, hotel security was there very quickly, or I may have been tempted to re-educate him.

These attitudes also applied to men, although not in such a harsh manner. We also had a tough time if we dared to wear running shorts inside or outside the hotel. The first time I went running, I had no idea that the sight of men's legs was so taboo. I was made aware of my transgression by the spitting and hissing of every man I ran past. I promptly returned to the hotel, never to go out running in that country ever again. I was even hissed at when I walked to the hotel gym in my running gear. Apparently, I should have got changed in the gym, not my room. I never made that mistake again.

That reminds me of a funny story on one flight to Saudi. On a previous trip, I had purchased six miniature bottles of wine on the aircraft to take home. I had placed these bottles in my case compartment and promptly forgotten all about them. Imagine my horror at opening the case in my hotel room in Saudi. I panicked. What on earth was I meant to do now? I trembled, realising the near miss I'd had. The thought of the consequences of customs opening my case on arrival was terrifying. I quickly emptied all the wine bottles down the sink and immediately let out a sigh of relief, which lasted until I looked at the six empty bottles sitting on the sink.

What on earth was I going to do now? If I left them in my room bin for the cleaners to find, I would be arrested either before I left the hotel or as soon as I arrived at the airport. No, I had to dispose of them quickly without anyone seeing me do it. I put them in my rucksack and set off to find a bin in the hotel. Ten minutes later, I returned to my room defeated; there was no bin to be found outside of my room. My six empty bottles and I sat down on my bed to rethink the whole problem. The solution suddenly hit me, go running. Not to admit my crime and go on the run, but rather to hide the bottles in my gym bag and go running on the treadmills in the gym. Next to each running machine were large bins for people to throw their small gym towels in after use. I grabbed six towels and quickly went to the nearest toilet cubicle. I carefully wrapped each bottle into one of the towels and replaced them in my bag. I spent the next hour on the running machine, only stopping to wipe my brow and dispose of the slightly heavy towel. Luckily, nobody noticed that I used six different towels. I quickly escaped after disposing of the last incriminating towel-wrapped bottle. I still wonder to this day what the workers in the laundry room made of those six bottles and if their subsequent disposal had, in fact, caused any problems for them. I genuinely hope not.

Kuwait was always one of my favourite destinations in the Middle East. It is a small, friendly and welcoming country. The airport station manager always greeted me by my first name and made all of us very welcome. The same happened at the hotel. The manager always made a point of greeting us personally. My runs in Kuwait were short by my usual standards. My route took me down to the harbour and back through the busy streets - only about five kilometres but enjoyable, nevertheless.

We always landed in the evening; too late to run. On my last trip to Kuwait, I was tying my shoelaces in the morning to prepare for my run. I heard a clap of thunder which was surprising as when I had looked out of the window only moments ago, there was not a cloud in the sky. Within two minutes, my bedside telephone began ringing, another unexpected and unusual occurrence. I was tempted not to answer it. I was ready to run, and I did not think that the call would be anything significant, probably one of the crew asking if I wanted to go for breakfast. Luckily, my curiosity got the better of me, and I picked up the phone. It was the hotel manager.

There had been a large bomb explosion in the vicinity of the hotel. He sounded close to tears as he asked me if my crew were all safe. He, more than anyone, should know that we do not all stay in the same room, so I replied that I had no idea. I reassured him that I would check and let him know. He gave me the crew's room numbers, and I started dialling. Twenty minutes later and all the team were accounted for, bar one. I called the manager back and informed him that one of our crew was unaccounted for. He asked the name of the missing person and when I told him, I was astounded that the manager knew him. Apparently, the crew member had once lived in Kuwait. The manager tracked him down, staying at a friend's house. We were all safe. I cannot think of another hotel manager who would go to those lengths to check on the safety of his guests.

The mood was very sombre as we checked out that night to fly home. Twenty-seven people had been killed just down the road from where we were staying. Another two hundred and twenty-seven had been injured. What made it even worse for us as a British Airways crew was that the suicide bomber had probably arrived on our flight the previous evening. We were all shocked and saddened to hear this news. I have no idea if this rumour was true or not. I never found the truth, but the thought that we had inadvertently brought death and destruction to that lovely country made my blood run cold and still haunts me to this day.

Chapter 15

The Land of the Free

My first trip as a 747 pilot to the United States was to New York. On that winter's day in 1987, I had no way of knowing just how big a part that city would play in my life over the coming decades.

I still vividly remember my first approach and landing at New York's JFK airport. I was flying the first generation of the Boeing 747; the 100 series. This aircraft was first commissioned in the 1960s. The technology, or lack of it, meant that every approach relied entirely on the pilot's skill. Mine had reached a barely competent level at that time, or so it felt. By the time I arrived at the hotel in Manhattan, I was a mental and physical wreck, far too tired to consider going for a run. I barely managed to summon up the energy to meet up for the customary beer in the evening.

Luckily, the following day, I felt very different. Although we only had twenty-four hours in the Big Apple, there was always plenty of time for that all-important run. The five-hour time difference between the East Coast of America and the UK meant that I was always awake around six in the morning, a perfect time to see the city. Over the decades, we moved hotels at regular intervals, although happily for me, they were all within an easy running distance from Central Park. What more could a runner possibly want?

Usually, I tried to avoid areas or routes that were popular with other runners. I preferred my own company when running. Over the years, friends and crew members have asked if they could run with me. I usually made excuses, anything, to avoid running with someone else. There are two main reasons for this. Firstly, it is difficult to find two people who can run at the same pace. Indeed, my own pace varies from day to day. If I accepted someone's request to accompany me, I would have to run at a much slower rate or, more commonly, at a much faster one. The other reason I prefer solitary running is that it is the only time I can be totally alone with my thoughts. Over the years, many of my best and, of course, many of my worst ideas germinated as I plodded along whichever route I followed. Running can do that to a person; it purges the mind of trivia, making space for new, hopefully inventive, original thought. Of course, I also had, and continue to have, many completely useless and unworkable ideas and inspirations. The critical thing was being alone. It allowed my mind time to empty, contemplate and recharge. In all honesty, the main reason I prefer solitude is that, embarrassingly, I possess a powerful sense of competitiveness. In other words, I cannot allow anyone to overtake me.

In my younger years, this was not too much of a problem. I could increase my pace if another runner appeared at my shoulder. Nowadays, the sight of a sixty-something-year-old trying to outpace a twenty-year-old is more comical than competitive. Yet to my great shame, I still strive to do it.

As I entered Central Park for the first time on that cold, grey December morning, I was greeted by hundreds of similar-minded people. All were happily engaged in running in an anti-clockwise direction around the park. New Yorkers started their day very early it appeared, as it was still barely light. Yet here they all were, all running their hearts out before they began work. My initial reaction was to run in the opposite direction, clockwise. After a few hundred yards and about a similar number of disapproving looks and comments, I turned around and followed the herd. Fortunately, I was slightly faster than most of my fellow runners. I managed to complete the route around the outside of the park without being overtaken. I had yet to realise that Central Park is not flat, far from it. I felt my running shoes had wings on the first part of the run. I was flying along, totally unaware that I was running down a gentle slope. The downside of running downhill was that you must go back up sooner or later if you run a circular route. As I rounded the outdoor swimming pool at the upper east side of the park, I was suddenly faced with over a mile of steeply inclined pathways. This was totally unexpected and caused my pace to slow noticeably. Suddenly, I found the other runners on my shoulders, who obviously knew about this steep climb. They, of course, were prepared for the climb and had been pacing themselves accordingly. On the other hand, I had raced my way along the route, cheerfully passing everyone else. How they must have laughed at this idiot running at full speed. They had let me pass them in the full knowledge that they would get their revenge very shortly.

I gritted my teeth and pushed on up the hill. I was determined that I would not be overtaken. The hill seemed to go on forever; the further up I went, the steeper it became. I was nearing the limit of my endurance as I approached the famous Dakota building and the Strawberry Fields. It was here that John

Lennon lived and sadly, died. Fortunately for me, it also spelt the end of the long, challenging climb. As the road levelled out, I regained my breath as the skyscrapers reappeared above the park's tree line. I was on my way back to the hotel, with only three kilometres to go. 'Thank God', I thought to myself, 'hopefully, no more hills'.

British Airways always favoured the midtown section of Manhattan when choosing the crew hotels and the majority of these were on or around Lexington Avenue. This meant a twenty-minute run through the busiest streets of New York on the way to and from Central Park. The route took me along 5th Avenue, past the Rockefeller Center, and up Park Avenue. Being British, I obeyed all the traffic lights. I spent most of my time apologising to people as I tried to make my way through the crowds of shoppers and tourists. The pavements had been relatively quiet on my journey to the park. However, the shops had now opened, and there was barely a spare inch of pavement on which to walk, let alone run.

I was now at a standstill, a runner trapped in a sea of shoppers. I hate, literally hate, stopping on a run. Sometimes, it is inevitable. Crossing busy roads or passing the Ferrari showroom on Park Avenue, you have no choice but to stop and admire the latest supercar. Frustratingly, there was no reason for me to be stationary in my present position. The sheer number of the crowds was forcing me to abandon my run. There had to be a solution if I was ever going to be a regular runner in this city. Looking around, suddenly, I saw the answer. On almost every road in Manhattan, a bike lane runs alongside it. There were many signs indicating that these were reserved for bikes only. There were big signs with a black cross over matchstick people every few hundred yards. These bike lanes were jealously guarded by the radical bike brigade. This was their territory and theirs alone.

I thought long and hard for nearly a minute before deciding that the pedestrian restrictions were just that, a restriction for pedestrians. On the other hand, I was a runner; petty by-laws did not apply to me. I was, above all that. I was simply a cyclist without a bike. And with that thought held firmly in my mind, I took my life in my hands and stepped into the world of the New York cyclist. I left the pavement and set off to catch the bike that had just passed me. I was now determined to avoid being overtaken by cyclists instead of other runners.

New York, being New York, nothing on the roads moved very quickly. Every few hundred yards, a junction appeared with the inevitable traffic lights. The traffic moved at a snail's pace. It was literally quicker to run around the streets than to drive. This also applied to cyclists. They had to stop at the next set as they accelerated away from one set of lights. This gave me a fantastic opportunity to race the bikers. A bike would overtake me, and I would reverse the process at the next light as I jumped onto the pavement and ran alongside the pedestrians as they crossed at the junction. Occasionally, I would even have the pleasure of overtaking the slower bikes between the lights. I had found my own system to run around New York. I was the cyclist with the invisible bike.

As my pace seemed to fit with the other traffic in the bike lane, not once over the next four decades, did I ever receive any reprimand for being in the hallowed bike lane. I was accepted. With this newfound freedom, I enjoyed running from one side of Manhattan to the other. I would run alongside the East River, following underneath the FDR driveway, looking across at Brooklyn. From there, I would pass underneath the magnificent Brooklyn Bridge and make my way towards the Statue of Liberty. Continuing my run would take me to the Hudson River and towards Battery Park. At this point, before 9/11, the Twin Towers would appear on the horizon. Passing the rows of piers with the cruise liners and the aircraft carrier *Intrepid*, it wasn't easy to believe that I was still in New York. From there, I would cut back into the city's heart, make my way back to midtown, and take a quick nap before flying back to London that night.

Over the decades, gradually, I fell in love with New York. I came to think of it as my city, which was crazy, as I lived only thirty miles from London. I knew New York like the back of my hand, yet on the rare occasions I took the train to London, I emerged from Victoria Station into an alien world. I took my eldest son, James, to New York on a number of occasions. On one trip, when he was just twelve years old, he asked if he could go for a walk while I grabbed a quick nap before our flight home. He left our hotel room with strict instructions not to be out for longer than thirty minutes. When I awoke an hour later, there was still no sign of James. I called his mobile phone, but there was no answer. I was due to go to work in an hour. Three hundred passengers were hoping to fly home with me that night. How could I fly them back to London and then explain to my wife that I had lost our son in New York City?

Fortunately, there was a timid knock at my door a couple of minutes later. Throwing open the door, there, to my huge relief, was James. I was about to demand an explanation when I noticed that James looked very upset. He had become lost, and his phone had run out of power. There was no point in scolding him further; he had learnt his lesson. What I hadn't realised that day, however, was that James had also fallen in love with New York.

Eleven years later, he returned to study at the New York Film Academy. His course was due to last just under a year. Ten years later, he has still to return from living in New York. Instead, he is happily married to his lovely wife, Carlotta. They are both incredibly successful and live in one of the areas I first ran in all those years ago. We love the fact that he is happy and prosperous in his choice of career and place to live. It does haunt me slightly that when that little twelve-year-old boy became lost in the big city, only a part of him came home to us. As he knocked on my hotel room door, unbeknownst to me, the seeds had been sown for his future. We still miss him daily and I am not sure Liz, has ever fully forgiven me for taking James on that life-changing trip.

I flew to New York more than any other American city. British Airways had twelve flights a day, operated mainly by the jumbo. There were many other cities that I enjoyed exploring with my running shoes. Boston was high on my list of running destinations. Leaving the hotel, I would make my way down to the James river, turn right and head for the Longfellow Bridge. Crossing over the bridge, I would turn left and head back along the river all the way to Harvard University. It was a glorious run in any season. Still, spring was always my favourite as the Canadian geese returned to breed along riverbanks. Winter could be brutal as the snowstorms made their way down from the Arctic. I have encountered some of the heaviest snow on my runs on that long route. The only city to rival Boston for heavy snow was the Windy City, Chicago.

Staying on the east coast but a world away from the harsh winter weather was Miami. Often in the same week, I could be slipping and sliding my way through an icy landscape in New York and then sweating along the waterfront in sweltering Florida. If you think it's hot in winter, try running in Florida during the summer months; it's brutal. On a run from Dadeland, just south of Miami, I headed off towards the coast some five kilometres away. The plan was to run to the beach, turn right, run along the Old Cutler road, turn back through a housing estate, and finally, through a large mall back to the hotel. I calculated this run's length at around eighteen kilometres, a challenging distance but hopefully manageable. How wrong I was.

I never, ever, take water on a run. The only time I tried it, I had shaken the water holder to within an inch of its life by the time I felt thirsty. This shaking produced kinetic energy, which in turn heated the water. As I took a mouthful of warm tepid water, it was like drinking a cup of coffee that had been left to cool for too long - not pleasant at all. I had started my run a little later than I usually did. We had been delayed on the flight from London, and we were seven hours behind our scheduled arrival time when we finally got to the hotel. After a long restorative sleep, I started my run at midday instead of the usual early morning. It was the middle of summer, and there was not a cloud in the sky. This should have provided clues as to the wisdom of attempting such a run in these conditions. The humidity was also close to one hundred per cent. The first part of the run went well. The road I was following took me away from the heavily populated area of Dadeland towards a very upmarket housing area. The further I went, the bigger the houses became, and the more I enjoyed daydreaming of being able to afford to live in such splendour.

After about forty minutes, I reached the coastline and turned right to follow an inland waterway. The scenery was stunning, and as I followed the track along this almost deserted pathway, I reflected on how lucky I was to run in such a beautiful part of the world. Before long, it was time to turn back towards Dadeland and through an even more spectacular housing estate. I really was now in the heart of the multi-millionaires row. As I stared enviously at each property and the Ferraris, Porches, and Bentleys parked outside, I realised that I was starting to feel unwell. My head suddenly felt like it wanted to explode, and my vision blurred. The sensible thing to do was to stop but this was not an option for someone as daft as me.

I tried running in the shade as much as possible to escape the burning sun. I was still about five kilometres from the hotel and was now in desperate need of water. There were no shops around until I reached the end of my run, just row after row, street after street of beautiful houses. I began to feel even worse, my pace had slowed to a trot, and I began to search for any sign of water. It dawned on me that there was literally no one else around, not a single person. I was lost in a sea of luxury with no way to find the water I so desperately craved. Desperate situations called for desperate measures, and I suddenly saw a water source. Just inside a driveway, a hose was automatically spraying a vast area of grass. I looked around, and there was no one in sight, so I decided to break the law and become a trespasser. Entering the garden, I reached down to try to stop the mechanical arm from throwing the precious water onto the lawn. As I attempted and failed to achieve this act of water theft, suddenly, I heard this thunderous and outraged voice asking me what I thought I was doing. This was an excellent question, one I would have asked had I caught a complete stranger standing in my front garden attempting to stop my hose from doing its job.

Anytime I got into a problematic situation in America, I tended to put on my best British accent and pleaded temporary insanity. It was surprising how often this worked. Luckily for me, today was one of those days. I apologised profusely. Sheepishly, I began to explain that my desperate need for water had caused me to intrude on his sprinkler system. The homeowner looked at me with an astonished look on his face as I described the route I had taken to get to his front garden. Instructing me to stay where I was and not to touch his water spraying system, he disappeared back into his mansion. This could go one of two ways: I was either going to get a drink, or I would shortly hear the sounds of sirens as the local police force descended on me. Having to cancel that evening's flight because the pilot was locked up in a local jail would not go down well with my employer. Fortunately, the very understanding homeowner reappeared carrying a large bottle of ice-cold water.

Freezing water is not the best thing to drink if you are dehydrated and suffering from heat exhaustion. The shock to the body as it experiences the two extremes of temperature can leave you feeling worse, not better. As I stumbled out of the driveway calling out both further apologies and thanks at the same time, I actually felt worse than I had before attempting my water heist.

Still, I had another five kilometres to go, so I tried to ignore my thumping headache and nausea. I still held on tightly to my gift of water and regularly stopped to take a sip. Slowly, as I progressed back to the hotel. with each step, the bottle was shaken, and good old kinetic energy began to warm the water. This, in turn, meant that each time I drank, the shock to my system was no longer as great as the previous one. By the time I reached the hotel, my water bottle was as empty as I felt. As I opened my hotel room door, I managed to make it to my bed before finally collapsing. I lay there trying to stop the room from spinning around. As my eyes began to focus once more, I looked at my watch. I had been running for over two hours in extreme heat and humidity. 'What an idiot', I thought to myself, as I closed my eyes and again fought against the room's tendency to rotate when I least expected it to.

Another favourite route was to run from downtown Miami along Brickell avenue and onto Virginia Key. After a hot run along the busy road, an underpass brought you out on the long route to the William Powell bridge in the far distance. The bridge was about half a mile long and included a steep climb as it rose to allow the superyachts to pass underneath. If anyone tells you that Florida is flat, they need to run up and down that bridge. The run itself was magical once you got away from the busy roads. Part of the route took you along a golden sandy beach where you could see the manatees or sea cows enjoying themselves if you were lucky enough. After the long climb over the bridge, you descended onto the key itself. A further smaller bridge took you onto the golf course at Key Biscayne. Simply a beautiful run, long but worth every step. Once around the golf course, it was time for the long run back to the city centre. I learnt to avoid flying to Miami in the summer. It really was too hot.

Chapter 16

A Burning Ambition

Denver, like San Francisco and a few other towns and cities in the US, have more than their fair share of homeless people. I have heard a few explanations for this sorry state of affairs over the years and I am in no position to know which one is correct. One of the more plausible theories was that these cities had a more liberal attitude toward supporting the homeless. However, after seeing just how wretched their lives are, I found it difficult to believe that these unfortunate individuals received any help at all.

On my first visit to Denver, I did as I always do: I studied a map and set off on what appeared to be a good running route. I planned to follow a path running alongside Cherry Creek, a waterway circumnavigating the city. As I left the hotel, I noticed a cardboard box or filthy sleeping bag at almost every shop front. On closer inspection, they were all occupied by some of the most unfortunate people I have ever seen. I have been to some of the poorest places on earth, so I knew what deprivation looked like. I am not easily shocked but to see these men and women trying to survive on these cold and lonely streets really shocked me. Many of the men appeared to be veterans who had once served their country in the armed forces. They still wore the rags that had once been part of their smart uniforms. Signs scribbled on damp cardboard gave details of their backgrounds. They had served in Vietnam, Iraq and Afghanistan. They had lost limbs, they had lost their livelihoods, and most heartbreakingly, they had lost their dignity.

Unlike in countries such as the UK, there was no safety net for these desperate people. In the wealthiest nation the world has ever known, there was nothing to stop you from tumbling down to the very bottom of society. Although people fall through the net and onto the streets in other first-world countries, at least there were nets to fall through. These homeless and desperate souls were moved on before the residents and shoppers drifted onto the streets, only for them to return on the late and usually cold nights. My early morning run took me past row upon row of temporary bedrooms until, with a sigh of relief, I reached the track that would take me along the creek. It was still very early, just after six in the morning, which to my body clock was early afternoon. I appeared to be the only runner-up so early. If this had been New York, I would have a multitude of fellow runners, but here, I was alone. I had my iPhone securely tucked away in a special pocket in my running shorts, just in case I got lost. This item was a luxury I could have only dreamed of when I first started running.

Thirty minutes later, the Denver skyline was merely an object in the distance as the creek finally turned to weave its way back to the city centre. Ahead of me, an eight-lane freeway made its way over the creek, creating a long underpass. As I entered this semi-dark tunnel, I quickly became aware of a large number of eyes following my every step. As my eyes adjusted to the low light level, I realised there were sleeping bags, abandoned shopping trolleys, and rubbish everywhere. I had entered a new underworld, one that I wanted to leave as quickly as possible. Did I continue running to the far end or turn around and leave hastily without further delay? Of course, I went for the least sensible option. My never-stop-never-turn-back mentality was about to get me into trouble again, but not for the reasons I expected.

The end of the flyover was no more than two hundred metres in front of me. I could see the light at the end of the proverbial tunnel. Numerous pairs of eyes now seemed firmly focused on me, and I felt very vulnerable and uncomfortable. I noticed people sitting against concrete pillars, and a few began to shout at me. Feeling very tense, I clenched my fists and broke into a sprint, at least my version of one. I felt a sharp burning pain in my right buttock at that precise moment. The pain was so sudden and intense that I let out a loud yelp while transitioning from one of the *Chariots of Fire* sprinters to a madman hopping along, clutching his backside.

My first thought was that someone had thrown a lump of hot coal from one of the numerous fires that were being used to keep these folk warm and make hot drinks. It was an uncharitable thought, and one that I was about to discover could not have been further from the truth.

I had not been attacked by the homeless of Denver. I had been assaulted by those folks in Silicon Valley, California. As my hand reached the back of my shorts, the pain was such that I considered pulling my shorts down to get some relief from the heat. Luckily for everyone concerned, I refrained from a public act of indecency. I now had everyone's undivided attention. I had located the source of the burning heat. My iPhone had literally gone into meltdown mode.

When a lithium battery lets go, it does so in a very spectacular manner. After pulling this melting mass of glass and plastic from my shorts, immediately, I dropped it on the ground. I stood in utter disbelief as the phone got hotter and hotter and began to buckle under the intense heat. I was quickly joined by a large group, equally amazed at what they were witnessing. We were all in this together. I was surprised at the technical knowledge of my newfound friends. They were all well-versed in the pros and cons of the latest version of the iPhone. Sadly, my iPhone was at least four years old and was one of the earliest models. There were disapproving looks all around whilst the virtues of the latest model were discussed in earnest; it was like playing a fiddle whilst Rome burnt. After about five minutes, which gave the onlookers plenty of time to deride my phone choice, I managed to stoop down and retrieve what was left of my prized possession. It was still far too warm to return it to its original position. Besides, my bottom was still smarting. Instead, I passed it from hand to hand like the roasted hot chestnuts we used to eat in winter and once again, set off to complete my run. As I burst out again into the bright sunlight, I could still hear the ringing echoes of advice regarding my poor phone choice and what I should buy next.

Later that day, I took my iPhone, or more accurately, the remains of my iPhone, into the local Apple Store. Holding up the charred remains, I asked, more in hope than expectation, if they could kindly replace the phone. Once again, my iPhone began to attract a sizable crowd, all eager to see what a wayward battery could do. Most of them had name badges declaring them to be geniuses of the modern hi-tech world. This claim seemed very questionable as soon as they opened their mouths. My new friends living under the freeway had a much tighter grip on reality and the cause of my iPhone dilemma than this group. Eventually, the head genius declared that the phone had overheated because I was running. I tried to explain that may be the case with a water bottle, but it was highly unlikely my running pace would cause a battery to implode. Had they seen me run?

Despite my insistence, the gaggle of geniuses declared that their leader was always correct, which is why he was the head genius. And with that declaration and collectively denying me a replacement, they began to lose interest in my melted phone. They wandered away to do what geniuses do.

Well, I was not having this, and besides, my bottom was still stinging. Nerdy genius notwithstanding, I stood my ground and demanded to see their manager. After a ridiculously long wait - I expect that they were hoping I would accept their final word, give up, and go away - the great man finally appeared. I put my case to him, and he began to ponder the situation. Holding the phone between two fingers, a little like people holding a dog poo bag after their pet had performed, he asked me if I ever sweated whilst running. Affirming that, of course, I did, he immediately declared that the phone had suffered water damage which resulted in the overheating. I was astonished. I wondered how this man had risen to lead a pack of geniuses who had magically reappeared to witness greatness in action. The verdict seemed signed, sealed and delivered until I pointed out that the temperature had been close to freezing whilst I was running and I never sweat at that temperature. Anyway, I was sure my bottom cheeks didn't sweat at any temperature. I dug my heels in. I wanted my phone replaced, and I wanted it replaced now.

He refused. It was a standoff, tech genius against a disgruntled runner with a smarting bottom! I had one more ace to play. I informed him that I would be suing Apple and immediately telling the press that their phones were unsafe and could cause serious injury. The manager sceptically questioned the fact that severe injury could result from an overheated phone. I pulled my jeans down on one side to reveal a nasty burn already weeping. Ten minutes later, I walked out of the store with a brand-new iPhone. Apparently, they no longer made the model I possessed. If I had stayed in Denver another day, I would have returned to the underpass to show everyone my new phone. Instead, I spent an uncomfortable night in the cockpit, flying home, trying not to put too much pressure on my right bum cheek.

Phoenix is another fascinating city to run in. If I had my career choice again, I would choose to be a weather forecaster in Arizona. I would record two forecasts and replay them as appropriate. I would stand in front of a giant map showing Phoenix and the surrounding area. On that map, I would have an equally massive symbol for the sun, and that would be that. In the first version, I would announce that the temperatures would be well above one hundred degrees, so take care. On the other version, the temperature may drop below one hundred degrees, so go out and enjoy yourselves. That done, I would take the rest of the year off.

Unfortunately, my real job involved a lot more work which occasionally necessitated me being in Phoenix on the hotter days of the year. I always seemed to miss the ten days of the year when it was actually bearable to go outside. I restricted my runs to five kilometres, such was the brutality of the heat. Over the years, I saw new shopping malls spring up and quickly close down again. It was so sad to see these huge empty buildings boarded up with weeds growing everywhere and tumbleweeds blowing across the endless empty car parks. This was just after 2008 and the global financial crash. There were also empty executive houses. For some reason, Phoenix seemed to be suffering far more than any other American city I visited. I never understood the reason for this, and it made my visits and runs in the city slightly sad. I tried to avoid flying to Phoenix unless it involved a game of golf in the marginally cooler winter season. Either that or they finally offered me a job as a weather forecaster.

I was in Las Vegas at the height of summer. Again, I decided to run as the sun came up to avoid the day's extreme heat. Our hotel was situated just off the famous strip. A six o'clock run in the morning would be a quiet time to enjoy the incredible sights without the crowds.

I am not, nor ever have been, a fan of gambling. It has nothing to do with principles, ethics or anything similar. It is just that gambling really does not interest me. I can see the skill required in some games, such as poker or blackjack. Still, the idea of feeding money into a flashing machine or placing a bet on a spinning wheel holds no attraction at all. But I am happy whiling away the occasional hour in a casino, watching other people lose their money whilst I take advantage of the free drinks on offer. What I still needed to appreciate about Las Vegas was that the gamblers gambled all night. Here I was, running along the strip at six o'clock in the morning, and people were still coming out of and entering the vast casinos. After a heavy night, they did not appreciate a runner trying to pass them by. So I took an unplanned deviation away from the bright lights. Once you left the bright lights of the strip behind, you very quickly entered a not-so-salubrious neighbourhood. I promptly got lost amongst the backstreets. Of course, I had a pretty good idea of which direction I needed to head to return, but by this time, the sun was fully up, and the temperature was soaring.

I began to feel some of the symptoms I had first experienced all those years ago in Dubai. I slowed down to conserve my energy and sanity and made a beeline for the hotel. I ran down a street that had seen much better days. By the look of things, so had the occupants and they had probably spent all their money in the casinos. They were sleeping in cardboard boxes and drinking spirits directly from the bottle. The contrast could not have been more extreme in such a short distance. Literally yards from where these wretched people tried to survive, gamblers lost more on one turn of cards than these desperate folk would see in a year. My mood darkened, and I felt tremendous sympathy for these homeless people. Maybe, if lady luck had smiled on them years ago at the gaming tables, they would be living in a high-rise apartment, not a bus shelter.

As I passed one poor woman lying next to a shopping trolley containing her worldly possessions, I noticed her suddenly sit up straight and look directly at me.

"Pick ya f***ing feet up and run properly, you f**ker," she yelled at me; not the words I was expecting to hear.

Looking down, I could see that she was absolutely right. I was shuffling along like an old man, not running like an athlete. I could not help but smile. I found the fact that she had taken a moment out of her wretched life to give me some running advice incredibly touching. I just wished that I had some money to give her. Sadly, I had forgotten to put some in my pocket before I set off. To this day, when I feel that I am shuffling rather than running, I think back to that poor woman and silently thank her. She still remains the only person ever to have given me such truthful and precise running advice.

Of course, I was shuffling because I had started again to experience heat exhaustion and dehydration. I had intended to run for thirty minutes and had been out for over an hour. As I eventually made my way into the hotel car park, I looked up at the colossal temperature display. Once again, I had run in over fifty degrees of heat. I still had to learn my lesson, and it would take yet another run to finally appreciate the dangers of heat.

Chapter 17

Texan Giveaway

Houston was a regular and delightful destination for me, mainly because my lifelong friend had emigrated there. Initially, we stayed in the Woodlands, an upmarket community just north of the city. Runs from here were glorious, along specially built paths which wound through creeks and golf courses. Everyone looked unusually happy. All in all, it was identical to the film, *The Truman Show*. Every time I went out, I expected to see Jim Carey waving to me and wishing me a good day. Like the film, it all eventually unravelled, and the company sent us to stay in downtown Houston, a real culture shock.

My last run in The Woodlands was the most memorable. Pete Brown, who had emigrated to Houston, had his fiftieth birthday quickly approaching. With a bit of subterfuge and planning, we had arranged with his wife to be there on his big day. I had not seen Pete for a few years and thought surprising him on his birthday would be fun. We arrived the day before and checked into a local hotel. Pete, at the time, was trying to regain his youthful physique with a daily run. It hadn't worked for me, but Pete was willing to give it a go. He followed the same route each day. We waited in our hire car until we received a message from his wife that Pete had set off. Liz dropped me off about one hundred metres behind Pete, and I set off after him, dressed in my running gear. I approached Pete, who was puffing a bit but I stayed just behind him. I had sunglasses on and had pulled a baseball cap down over my forehead. My mother would have had difficulty recognising me.

I sat on Pete's shoulder. He looked around and tried to accelerate away, but I stayed with him. Putting on what was probably the worst Texan accent in the history of accents, I called out for the fat old git in front of me to get the hell out of the way and let a real runner get past. The old Pete, or should that be younger Pete, would have stopped and thumped me. Living in America must have softened him up as this time, he stood aside. As I overtook him, I gave him an almighty shove and said along the lines about old men clogging up the roads. This brought the Pete I knew back to life. I managed to whip my cap and sunglasses off before he could place a well-deserved punch on my chin. We had a great time once he had forgiven me.

Initially, I was bitterly disappointed at our hotel move. We were leaving a beautiful hotel in an idyllic location to a three-star motel next to an eight-lane freeway. I could hardly believe the difference between the two places. I promised myself not to be such a frequent visitor in the future. However, I still had a run to do, so I set off with little hope of an enjoyable experience ahead. Turning right out of the hotel, I ran alongside the elevated freeway and then along the main road. From Google maps, I had identified Memorial Park, a green area in a sea of concrete. Twenty minutes later, I crossed another main road and suddenly found myself in woodlands similar to the ones I had so enjoyed in the previous hotel. Following this path, I found myself running around a lovely golf course. I could feel the smile widening with each mile I ran. After an hour, I was heading back, having thoroughly enjoyed a run that initially, I had little enthusiasm for. It was now mid-morning, and I was feeling a little hungry. I had not eaten since landing the previous evening. As I approached the hotel, I noticed a huge shopping mall on the other side of the elevated freeway. Deciding that there must be an underpass nearby, I ran past the hotel seeking a way to cross over towards the shopping area. Just five minutes later, I found a pedestrian crossing. I still had a six-lane road to cross, and I waited patiently for the lights to change. Eventually, I managed to cross over the first three lanes. In the middle of the road, there was an area to wait whilst you waited for the next set of lights to change.

Standing there was a middle-aged man holding a large sign to attract the attention of the drivers waiting at the traffic lights. Next to him was a scruffy little dog lying loyally next to him. I bent down to stroke this friendly little bundle of fur and received a very warm reception. I looked at his owner as he stood precariously in the middle of the stationary traffic. He was dressed in a suit that had seen much better days. His face was hauntingly drawn and haggard, making him seem much older than he probably was. His sign gave some idea of his plight. It read simply, 'Please help me save enough money to buy a bike so I can cycle to work as a gardener'.

The last part of my run had taken me through an imposing area of huge executive houses set in their own large plots. The lights were taking forever to change, and I spoke to this poor man. His story nearly had me in tears. He had lived in one of these houses only a few months earlier. Sadly, he had lost everything as a drug habit stole his life away. He had hit rock bottom, and all he had left was his dog. Everything else from his previous life had been taken away from him. He explained that he had always loved gardening and that if he had a bike, he could hopefully start to rebuild his life.

At this point, the lights changed to green and with a final pat on his dog's head, I continued on my way. Ten minutes later, I stood outside a giant superstore, selling just about everything you could imagine. As I stepped inside, the first thing that caught my eye was a flash sale. And when I say flash sale, I mean flash sale. In front of me was a row of bicycles that had been reduced from four hundred to ninety-nine dollars. This sale was for four hours only, and there were only ten minutes left before they were due to return to their original price. Well, if this wasn't a sign, I don't know what was! Never before or since had I experienced such a coincidence. Here was a real chance to make a difference to someone down on their luck, and at ninety-nine dollars, it was a price worth paying.

Twenty minutes later, I recrossed that underpass, this time cycling, not running. I stopped in the same place to stroke the scruffy little dog whilst his owner again battled with the traffic. As he stepped back onto the pavement, I asked him if he could hold the bike whilst I stroked his dog. He readily agreed, and I continued to make a fuss of his dog. The lights changed from red to green. I stood up and started to run back to the hotel. He called out to me that I had forgotten my bike. I stopped, turned around and called back that I didn't own a bike, but he did now. I didn't wait for a reply. Instead, I turned and continued on my run.

When I got home two days later, I recounted this episode to Liz. I thought she might agree that it was good thing to have done. Instead, she rightly pointed out that now he had a bike, what on earth was he going to do with his dog? He could hardly cycle around balancing gardening tools and a dog on his handlebars. Damn, why hadn't I thought of that? I truly hope that I didn't make that lovely little dog homeless as well.

Chapter 18

California Dreaming

Onto the West coast and three of the places I loved to run; Los Angeles, San Francisco and Seattle. They were all memorable and enjoyable in their own ways. If I had to nominate one of these three as my absolute favourite, it would be the city by the bay, but more of that later.

Los Angeles is not a city; it is a vast expanse of humanity burgeoning out over a huge area. The heart of this metropolis itself is reasonably compact, with one main drag and a plethora of side streets radiating outwards. Main Street is like any other main street in the States. It contains all the luxury shops you could ever want. Wander off the main drag, and very quickly, you find yourself faced with the twin problems of poverty and crime. In no other city I have visited in America have I seen abject poverty and wealth so closely situated together. On the rare occasions we stayed in downtown LA, I ran with one eye in the back of my head if I left the main areas.

Luckily, we were normally accommodated in such places as Santa Monica, Manhattan Beach or Long Beach. I would set off from each of these locations and run along a beachfront path. Running in Los Angeles was obligatory, as far as I could see. The trails were full of toned, well-muscled athletes running at a pace I could only dream of. The men were pretty good as well! I would join in and try my best not to look too out of place. My strength was that I could run long distances at a reasonable pace. My fellow runners seemed to run at a fast speed for a short distance and then slow down or stop. I tried desperately to keep up with everyone on my first few runs. Experience quickly taught me that if I struggled to overtake another runner, it was best to wait until they slowed or stopped, which was much easier than all this racing nonsense.

The run along the seafront at Long Beach was especially interesting. Leaving the hotel in the centre of town, I would run in front of the enormous conference centre and make my way towards the beach. Here, I would pass a small harbour containing some great places to eat and drink. To the right lay *The Queen Mary*, the once great ocean liner, sadly now a static tourist attraction. Her funnels marked the start and finish line on my long run - not a bad reference point. Out to sea, you could make out Catalina Island, and in front of me, the sands of Long Beach, aptly named, stretching as far as the eye could see. I would set off heading for my first landmark, Belmont Pier, some five kilometres in the distance. A concrete path weaved its way along the perimeter of the beach, making an ideal cycling and running track. Often when running, I would have to spend the majority of the run looking at where I was placing my feet. This was especially true if, like me, you had very large feet that made a habit of finding any slight undulation in the path, a tree root, or rock to trip over and send the unwary flying through the air. Here, I could forget about untoward lumps and bumps, enjoy the smooth track and concentrate on the stunning scenery. Passing Belmont Pier, I would continue towards the peninsula. This signalled the end of the beach, and I would turn inland for the return leg. This time, the route took me along Ocean Drive, and most of the time, I could look down at the beach and the path I had just run along. Halfway home, there was a life-size bronze statue of a sailor from the Second World War. He stood looking out to the Pacific Ocean with a duffel bag slung casually over his shoulder. It was sobering to think of the number of these men who set sail from this very spot, never to return.

Another thirty minutes and the three funnels of *The Queen Mary* quietly slipped back into view, signalling the end of a fulfilling run. It was probably pouring down with rain at home, and here I was, struggling to put my running top back on before going into the hotel.

Seattle in the north provided a similar but very different coastal run. For one thing, the weather here was more like running in the UK than on the west coast of America. In other words, it rained a lot. Flying into Seattle was always special. This is where the Boeing 747, the aircraft I had been fortunate enough to fly for a world record thirty-four years, was made. I was bringing my aircraft home. Depending on the landing direction, we often flew directly over Boeing Field. I often felt that the jumbo knew where she was and would reward me with an extra smooth landing as a thank-you for bringing her home.

The city itself lies on the coast and is a mainly industrial harbour. Giant cruise ships docked snugly alongside the fishing and sightseeing boats. The extensive waterfront contained a plethora of shops and eateries. From the city centre, it was difficult to access this coastline. You had to cross a freeway and descend steep steps before you could get down to the waterfront. I would always make my way to the famous Pike Place market. Here, the day's fresh catch was sold off in a very theatrical manner. I had never seen giant fish tossed around with quite such abandon; it was more of a show than a fish market, but the fish were sold in vast numbers, so the exhibition was profitable. Turning right, I would make my way past a small coffee shop called Starbucks. Apparently, they opened this shop in 1971 and hoped to expand to nearby cities. I thought it seemed to have worked out quite well for them as I left the city behind me.

Ten minutes later, I entered Myrtle Edwards Park, a narrow stretch of land containing many wonderful Eskimo carvings and statues. This was a gentle reminder of how far north we were. All too soon, the park ended at a massive industrial port. To get any further, you had to cross a hectic road and bridge before descending back onto a path on the other side. I did this once, but the hassle of making this crossing made it highly unattractive. Instead, I broke a habit of a lifetime and turned around and ran back the way I had come. The only consolation was that I could run on a different path on my way back through the park. The whole run was around eight kilometres - not far but enjoyable enough.

On one occasion, I decided to head to Lake Union, where I had heard rumours that a floatplane company, Kenmore Aviation, would allow British Airways pilots to sit in the spare pilot's seat if there was space available. I duly turned up, sweating after a ten-kilometre run. I produced my flying licence to the receptionist; sure enough, there was an empty seat next to the pilot. I set off in an amphibian Twin Otter, proudly sitting in the co-pilot's seat. The pilot and I were soon firm friends, and he even allowed me to fly the aircraft on sectors where there were no passengers. I loved it and flying around Victoria Sound and landing on small lakes was some of the most exciting flying I have ever experienced. All the pilot wanted to do was ask me about flying the 747. On the other hand, I only wanted to know about flying the Twin Otter. We parted at the end of the day as firm friends, each wishing for a short time that he could do the other person's job.

Chapter 19

Where I Left My Heart

At the beginning of my long career, I spent many months living and flying in San Francisco. I was paying for my flight training and flying in America was much cheaper than the UK. When I finally returned to England, I had left part of my heart behind. I had met someone special. Six years later, I returned as a first officer flying the Boeing 747, something I could have never imagined when I left San Francisco all those years previously.

And so I found myself back in the city that had played such a large part in my flying career and had bruised my young heart. As we made that first approach and landing, memories flooded back. The airport itself was very unusual in the way it handled inbound flights. You flew overhead the airport at ten thousand feet and then either turned left or right to start a rapid spiral descent before turning back to land on one of the two parallel runways. This resulted in a spectacular view of the Bay Area. The Golden Gate Bridge stood out, as did the San Mateo Bridge. Alcatraz was also very easy to identify, especially if the air traffic controller turned you left.

And here I was, back in San Francisco, but this time, I was being paid instead of paying to fly. I had the time to go running, something I could not afford to do the last time I was here. We always stayed in the city centre, usually around Union Square. This meant that I could plan my runs to take in all the sights and sounds of the city, and oh my goodness, what spectacular sights they were. All my routes would start the same way; an interesting level run along the always-crowded Market Street towards the ferry terminals. This is one of the few cities where I was able to run alongside a tram, what fun!

Upon reaching the ferry terminal, you crossed over the busy road and turned left towards the famous Fisherman's Wharf. I only recently discovered the meaning of Wharf, an acronym meaning Warehouse At River Front. Another useless fact to add to the mountain of them I have collected over the years. Running alongside the bay, you passed the vast piers and warehouses, most well past their prime but somehow, all the more interesting for that. You could peer into the cavernous interiors, once a hive of activity, now home to a few cars. The pavement was wide at this point, and I noted the increasing number of tourists as I ran past each warehouse. And then, I began to see the start of Fisherman's Wharf. Usually, many other runners enjoyed this route. It was a flat and reasonably easy run. On this occasion, I was running the shorter of the three routes I had been running over the years. The total distance was just over ten kilometres, but it's not the distance that was important on this run. It's what was to come as I turned back towards the city that was quite extraordinary.

As I passed Fisherman's Wharf, Alcatraz made an appearance sitting in splendid isolation in the middle of the bay. Obviously, the crowds were starting to build at this point, and I had to take care not to knock the tourists flying as I tried to enjoy the view while running. This was one of the best views of any run, and then there was the icing on the cake as I left the crowds behind and entered Crissy Field Marsh. This was parkland with well-marked out tracks, and from here, I caught my first glimpse of the Golden Gate Bridge. What more could anyone ask for on a run? At this point, I could turn left to return or carry on towards the bridge. I turned left towards Russian Hill, and when they said hill, my goodness, they really meant hill.

Those of a certain age may remember the television series *The Streets of San Francisco*, which often involved a car chase over the famous humps of Telegraph Hill and its connecting roads. Steve McQueen, in the iconic movie *Bullitt,* also had trouble keeping his Ford Mustang from becoming airborne as he hit the undulating roads. I also had difficulty navigating these streets but for an entirely different reason.

At first, the climb away from the waterfront was not too steep, but it certainly got the heart thumping. Still, I always enjoyed a challenging uphill run. As I approached Russian Hill, the topography really kicked in. Here, the climb ratio was around one in three. In other words, for every three feet, you went forward you would go up a foot. This was mountaineering, not running. This was not going to beat me, I refused to give in, and so I put my head down and pushed with every ounce of strength I had left in what was now my very tired legs. My arms pumped, and my lungs were nearly bursting; still, I pushed on. I could see the brow of the hill. 'Not too far to go', I kept reassuring myself.

As I continued, suddenly, I noticed something very strange. Although I was running as fast as I could for the conditions, the scenery around me stubbornly refused to change. That Volkswagen Beetle a hundred feet in front of me still appeared to be a hundred feet in front of me two minutes later. The houses on either side of the road had stayed the same. What on earth was happening? Had I entered a parallel universe? And then, an elderly lady came up behind me and asked if I could move out of the way. Stepping sideways, she passed me, walked up a flight of steps, and let herself into her apartment.

For the second time in my life, I had again, literally, run myself to a standstill, incredibly, without even realising it. Although my arms were still pumping away, my legs had given up the whole idea of forward movement. They had simply given up on me. I must have looked like a mime artist when they hit an invisible glass door. I was doing a good impression of a runner but without the forward momentum bit. I felt and also, certainly looked like a complete idiot. It is the only time in my running career when I have had to start walking in order to stop running. Well, I had already stopped; it was only my arms that were pretending I was still running.

After a short while, I attempted to set off running once again. Sadly, the difference in speed between the two was negligible, so I gave in and walked the rest of the way up the hill. In truth, as my running pace was slower than my walking speed, I was worried that the old lady would come out of her flat and overtake me again. I could just about handle being overtaken if I was walking, but to be overtaken again whilst running would have been too much for my ego. Running down the other side of the hills was, surprisingly, almost as tricky. Such was the gradient; it was challenging not to let your head get too far in front of your body. Once that happened, and you started to accelerate, it was almost impossible to stop. It was a little like tripping up and staggering forward while trying to keep your balance. Eventually, I managed to return to the hotel after sixteen fun-filled kilometres and four not quite so much fun ones.

As we had two clear days off on a west coast trip, I decided to run again but to cut out the embarrassing bits. I set off on one of my more adventurous routes, I was going to run all the way to Sausalito, and I was going to do it the pretty way. The route I had planned was the same as the day before, except as the Golden Gate Bridge came into view, I would continue towards it rather than run back into the city. I enjoyed all the sights of the previous day but instead of turning left up the dreaded hill, I continued through the park. From there, I ran up the steep path that winds its way towards the entrance to the bridge. I had calculated that the total distance would be around twenty-five kilometres to get to Sausalito. Obviously, running back again would be more than a little daunting, especially with those hills and that old lady waiting to humiliate me again. No, I would run there and break a habit of a lifetime and get a taxi back. All thoughts of the return journey were banished as soon as I took my first step onto the bridge.

Apart from the stunning views, I had yet to appreciate just how long the bridge was. The total distance was around three kilometres, but as far as I was concerned, it could have been thirty. Such was the thrill of running across the bridge; all sense of time and distance vanished. The weather was cool and windy. Luckily, the visibility was endless. Due to the weather, the bridge was relatively quiet that day. On many subsequent runs, the crowds made it impossible to run at the more congested points. The bridge's sheer size and majestic presence made me feel very small and humble as I made my way across. To the right, lay Alcatraz once again, this time framed by the city's outline, itself rising out of the ocean - beautiful, just beautiful.

All too soon, I was coming to the end of the bridge and what appeared to be the end of the pedestrian path. I could not continue without running alongside the freeway, so that's what I did. Initially, I found myself in a rest and observation area. I had hoped for a pathway down the hill to Sausalito, but there was no pedestrian access. Apparently, if you want to go to Sausalito from the Golden Gate Bridge, you did what all good Americans did, you drove.

Not having that option, I set off alongside the eight-lane highway, expecting at any moment, to be arrested for jaywalking, apparently, a serious offence. I had my best English accent at the ready should I have to explain myself to the local sheriff. Luckily, I got away without having to use stupidity as my defence plea. After about ten minutes, I managed to turn right and follow the steep twisting road down towards Sausalito. Again, there was no pedestrian pavement, and I had to take my chances with the oncoming traffic. Thirty minutes later, I finally arrived in the town itself. It was a welcome return after many years away. During my flight training all those years ago, I had stayed in Sausalito. The house I lived in appeared to have been replaced by a new apartment block; otherwise, very little had changed. The bars and restaurants on the quayside still held that very laid-back, almost bohemian atmosphere. Immediately, I felt at home. The years slipped away as I stopped and looked around. And then, I realised that I still had to make my way back to the hotel. I was flying home that night.

This is the only run I have ever done where I used another form of transport, apart from my feet, to get back to where I started from. The run had taken over two hours, and the crew bus was due to pick me up later that afternoon. I had to think of some other form of return transport, or I would delay the flight. Originally, I had thought of getting a taxi back, but somehow that seemed inappropriate now. I could see the city outline in the distance as I stood on the quayside. A mist was starting to descend and blur the horizon. The image of the city was fading in and out as the visibility began to reduce. Very quickly, all signs of San Francisco had disappeared, and a lonely foghorn started to emit its eerily echoing warning to the local seafarers. A shiver ran through me, and the temperature dropped noticeably. I felt a cold, wet blanket of fog enveloping me. As I continued to stare across the bay, a large vessel emerged slowly from the mist. All concept of distance was distorted as the vessel docked about one hundred metres from where I was standing. As I stood transfixed, ghostly figures emerged and made their way down the gangplank. It took me a little while to realise that this was the ferry that connected Sausalito with San Francisco, the perfect way to continue my journey, if my very unsteady sea legs could manage it.

With the decision made, I hurried towards the jetty where the boarding seemed to be taking place and joined a long line of people with bicycles, waiting to board. It didn't take me long to realise that everyone else had already purchased their tickets from a dockside office. Leaving the line, I hurried off to find this office and buy a ticket; easier said than done. Could I find the ticket office? Why hide a ticket office where nobody, well me, at least, could find it? Twenty minutes later, clutching my precious boarding pass, I was literally the last to board. The fog still clung stubbornly to the ferry and the surrounding buildings as I began to shiver.

I realised just how cold it had become. There I was in a vest and running shorts, whilst everyone around me was dressed far more appropriately. Still, the thought I consoled myself with, it was only a short crossing as the ferry moved slowly away from the quay and into the deepening gloom. I was beginning to regret my hasty decision to make a seaborne return to San Francisco. The vessel's foghorn sounded continuously as we made our way through the blanket of fog. There was no visibility at all. We seemed to be entirely alone in a sea of nothingness. I was now really, really cold. I stood there shivering. My post-run sweat had now helped to reduce my core temperature even further. I was not in a happy place. And then, as if by magic, everything changed.

One moment, it was like standing in a dark, gloomy room, and suddenly someone turned all the lights on and shone a spotlight on me. The ferry emerged from the tendrils of the fog bank into bright sunshine. The contrast from one moment to the next was stark. A moment earlier, I had been shivering in the gloom. The next, I was bathed in warm sunlight. As the temperature rose, so did my spirits as I watched the outline of the city get closer and closer. By the time we were disembarking,

I was ready for the five-kilometre run back along Market Street and up the steep hill back to the hotel. As I checked my watch, I realised I had run over twenty-five kilometres, a reasonable distance considering the hilly nature of the terrain. I made it back to the hotel with an hour to spare before pick-up, probably a little too close for comfort.

My other local route involved a long run in the opposite direction to the one I normally took. I was now heading towards Lincoln Park and Land's End Lookout. I was already beginning to regret my choice of route. Running along the increasingly downbeat streets was not a lot of fun. As I reached the coast, all that changed. Turning right, back towards the Golden Gate, I joined a route that took me along a spectacular coastline pathway. The beaches were vast and golden, something I had not expected. It wasn't easy to believe that I was still in the city, especially when the pathway took me through an area of beautiful seaside villas. This was more Malibu than San Francisco. Eventually, the bridge came into sight, and I turned back towards the city. Another run was done and one that, despite the coastal element, I was not to repeat. Those rundown areas I had to run through to get there were too depressing.

Chapter 20

Tragedy in the Heat

Vancouver, on the West Coast of Canada, is a wondrous destination for anyone who loves the great outdoors. The area enjoys its own unique microclimate at the base of the Rocky Mountains. It is also on the coast which adds to its allure. When I say micro, I really mean micro, but more about that later.

Flying into Vancouver was always great fun, especially on a cold, clear winter's day. Passing Whistler Mountain on the right-hand side, you descended over the endless range of the Rocky Mountains with their snow-capped peaks, a really inspiring panoramic vista. Although Vancouver is on the west coast, we only had twenty-four hours in the city. This was undoubtedly tough on my body clock, especially considering an eight-hour time change from the UK. Despite this, Vancouver offered one of the great runs and, sadly, one of my most tragic ones.

By the time we arrived at the hotel, it was late afternoon, around four in the morning at home. After an eleven-hour flight, I struggled with the idea of running on the day of arrival. Instead, it was an early night and an even earlier morning start. By six in the morning, I was ready for my run. We changed hotels over the years, but luckily, I could still complete the same run with just a few minor adjustments.

Setting off, I turned left onto Burrard Street and headed off towards Sunset beach. This took me away from the city on a busy road with wide pavements, allowing me to enjoy the views without dodging the crowds. From here, the run took me down a steep grassy slope onto a waterside track. English Bay provided the stunning background to Sunset Beach. At this point, there were still nearly twenty kilometres before finally, I would return to the hotel. So, I settled into my long-distance pace. Luckily for me, there were very few other runners at this time of the morning. I could choose my own pace without having to worry about being overtaken. Twenty minutes later and I was approaching the famous Stanley Park. There was an outdoor swimming pool for those hardy souls brave enough to battle the normally cool or cold temperatures. Passing the pool, I entered the park, well, more of an island than a park. If you can imagine Central Park in New York and then transfer the whole thing and attach it to the coastline of Vancouver, then you will have a rough idea of what Stanley Park was like. The path I was running on took me around the circumference of the park, the ocean on my left, and steep cliffs leading up to the park on my right. This was running heaven, a truly spectacular run with ever-changing views and weather.

Running along Sunset Beach and the first part of Stanley Park, the weather was mild, with a gentle breeze and clear skies. Just over halfway around the park, the track took you from one side of the bay to the other. Here, the weather was funnelled through a relatively small gap and created its own microclimate. One moment you were running in the warm sunshine; the next, the wind and the rain were battering you as you put your head down to grind through the adverse weather. As the pathway continued around the park, you began to head back towards the city. This weather phenomenon disappeared as quickly as it arrived. You were left wondering if it really happened at all.

All thoughts of the weather soon vanished as the city skyline came into view. With its narrow pathway, Brockton Point Lighthouse marked the beginning of the transition from sea views to city outlines. The path became broader and more crowded at his point, mainly with tourists out for a stroll. The main entrance to the park, marked with the traditional totem poles, appeared on the left. This was a great place to watch the many seaplanes begin their take-off rolls or bump down onto the water after their sightseeing tours of Victoria Island and beyond. As if that was not enough, the Naval Museum and the Royal Vancouver Sailing Club came into view with their magnificent clubhouse. From here, the run took you back towards the swimming pool and then left towards the city shoreline.

Running alongside the numerous small boats, waterborne bars, and restaurants, you were now well and truly back in the city. The pathway now climbed steeply past the seaplane terminal and towards the main shopping areas. Finally, a turn to the right took you onto Burrard Street once again and the final few kilometres back to the hotel. The total distance was just under twenty-five kilometres, so much contrast in such a relatively short distance.

Of course, you could run the route in the opposite direction, and I varied the order with each run. This time, I set off towards the seaplane terminal and into the park from the lighthouse side. It was the middle of summer and an abnormally hot day. I had set off much later than usual. We had had a lengthy delay the night before, and I woke up much later than usual. Still, this was a less of a problem than in some of my other runs. The temperature was only approaching thirty degrees, almost cool, as I set off. I passed the lighthouse and began to leave the crowds behind. I settled into my usual long-distance pace. The views, as always, held me spellbound as I continued out onto the almost deserted side of the park. I was at peace with myself and the world until I heard the phrase no runner ever wants to hear, "Excuse me."

I was listening to soothing music on my earbuds, so the phrase had to be repeated before I heard it correctly. The path at this point was at its narrowest, which made overtaking difficult. I was stunned. Had I been going so slowly that I was being overtaken? This was my worst nightmare. Did I move over, or did I accelerate away and leave this person spitting dust in my trail? Obviously, one of these elite athletes was about to leave me doing just that. I knew there were many better and faster runners than me. And so, I did the honourable thing and moved aside to let this Olympian go on their way.

As I moved over, I was crestfallen to see a middle-aged man with a big tummy, puff and pant his way past me. Well! As far as I was concerned, this was a red rag to a bull. I had never been beaten by such a runner before, and today was not going to be the first time.

I still had over fifteen kilometres to run and wanted to avoid being caught in the trap I often encountered in places like Central Park. There, I would battle against another runner only to find that they turned off after a short distance, leaving me panting like an idiot with another ten kilometres to run. Here, in Stanley Park, there were no escape routes, except at the halfway point, where there was a small beach and a refreshment area. No, this podgy runner was going the distance. He had thrown down the gauntlet, and there was no way I was going to let him get away with his "excuse me." This was war.

I quickly set off after him as he passed, me. Very soon, I was sitting right on his shoulder. I knew the pathway would open out, allowing me to overtake him without the need to ask. And that's precisely what happened. I passed him relatively quickly, and with a huge inward sigh of relief, I settled back into my run, albeit at a greater pace than before. 'Cheeky sod', I thought, as a self-satisfied smile spread across my face. And then, he overtook me again!

'How the hell did that happen?' I thought to myself. Unbelievably, he started to pull away from me. Swearing profusely under my breath, I put my head down and set off after him once again. This man was beginning to really annoy me. Again, I pulled up onto his shoulder and settled down at his increased pace. The pathway had narrowed once more, so I had to wait before attempting to overtake him again. I could hear him coughing and spluttering from this position, fighting for breath in the heat. Part of me began to feel sorry for him, and I thought of slowing down and letting him go. I did consider it until he tried to outrun me again. The pathway widened, and I overtook him for the second time. Immediately, he increased his pace, and we were now neck and neck. We ran as fast as we could, more like a couple of school children than two middle-aged men in silent but very real competition.

His breathing was now very laboured, and I began to have doubts as to the wisdom of continuing the race. Also, I was exhausted and still had fifteen kilometres to go. I slowed to my normal pace and let him disappear around the sharp bend ahead. Initially, I was crestfallen at being beaten. Still, I cheered myself up with the thought that he was probably running a much shorter total distance than I was attempting. And then, I came around the last corner before the beach and rest area.

In front of me was an ambulance with its red lights flashing and a crowd gathered around a prostrate figure lying motionless on the floor.

'Please, God', I thought to myself, 'don't let it be the runner I had been competing against'. I stopped to look. I was stunned and horrified when I recognised my opponent lying there. He was receiving electric shock treatment from the paramedics using a defibrillator. From the look on their faces, the prognosis did not look good. Apparently, the ambulance was there to treat an elderly tourist with a heat stroke. The runner had come around the corner and literally collapsed right in front of the ambulance.

I could obviously do nothing except feel a bit like a murderer. I turned away as they loaded the runner into the ambulance and sped away. It was a prolonged and challenging run back to the hotel. I never found out the fate of that poor man. I hope that he survived and made a full recovery. I learned a very valuable lesson that day and have never again tried to do such a stupid and immature thing as a race against someone who wants to overtake me. There is no need; let them go ahead.

Life is literally, too short.

Chapter 21

Missing the Boat

And so to Toronto, another favourite city of mine, a long way from Vancouver but just as enjoyable. The city sits on one of the Great Lakes, Lake Ontario, opposite Niagara Falls. One of the lesser-known facts about Toronto is that it has the longest Main Street of any city in the world, Yonge Street. This street ran for an incredible fifty-six kilometres. It featured in all of my runs, though obviously, I didn't run the whole length.

Instead, Yonge Street took me from the crew hotel down towards the lakefront. From here, I would take the ferry across to Toronto Island and another running paradise. Three ferry routes run to the island, one to each end, Harlan's and Ward and one to the middle of the island, Centre Point. Whilst having taken all three ferries, I preferred to set sail for Hanlan's Point and run to the other two ports. After leaving the ferry, I set off towards the small airport on the island's western side. It quickly became apparent that this was a very special place. As you left the small dock, there were an abundance of picnic areas and an almost complete lack of traffic. No vehicles, except a few essential services, were allowed, making it perfect for walking, cycling and of course, running.

Leaving the dock, there were two possible pathways to take. I always chose one for the outward run and the other for the return. The first path took you towards the sandy dunes, which thankfully, hid the nudist beach on the other side. I have always wondered why the people who really needed to keep their clothes on are the ones who flocked to these beaches. Still, luckily for me, everyone in sight seemed to have some form of clothing on. Leaving the beaches behind, I set off for Gibraltar Point with its lighthouse and craft school. This was still a relatively quiet part of the island. The tourists headed for Centerville and its Amusement Park. Luckily, I could avoid the crowds by staying on the track along the coast. As I approached the middle of the island, there were more sandy beaches, fortunately, this time for people who preferred to wear swimming attire. And then, onto the longest boardwalk, I have ever run along. This wooden pathway took me along the sea wall on one side and to the sand dunes on the other. Looking out across the lake, seals basked on the many rocks, a serene vista as I plodded on towards the far end of the island, Wards.

This is where the majority of the residents of the island lived. As I left the boardwalk, I entered an enchanting village of small wooden clapperboard houses. Each house was highly individual, some quite rundown, others obviously the apple of their owner's eye. Some places would appear to be holiday homes; others were permanent homes, and all were enchanting in their own way.

After running through the village, I passed the small Wards Dock before heading back towards the island's centre. I ran past the smallest fire station I had ever seen. Its one solitary fire engine glistened in the morning sunshine. Small boats bobbed on the inlets adding to the whole small island feel. The crowds got thicker as I ran through the middle once again before heading back to Hanlan's Point for the return ferry back to the city. This time, I took the lower pathway and passed the much larger boats moored along the quayside. The whole run was just over ten kilometres. Although it was a relatively easy run, there were no hills and, luckily, well-maintained pathways. Despite this, it was still a great run.

The only time I found it really challenging was on one particular winter's day. The weather was terrible, with heavy rain, sleet, and strong winds. I should have realised my mistake in going to the island when I saw that I was one of only a very few passengers on the ferry. Fifteen minutes later, and feeling seasick, I left the ferry. I ran into one of the most substantial headwinds I had ever encountered. The weather had yet to finish with me. In fact, it had hardly started to have its fun. As I approached the lakefront and boardwalk, giant waves crashed against the sea wall covering me in spray. As I approached Wards Dock, the rain and sleet turned into snow and hail.

Somehow, the wind had managed to reverse its direction and was now slamming ice particles painfully into my face. No one else was in sight as I made my way through the centre part of the island and headed back towards Hanlon Point and the ferry home. As I made my way towards the dock, I saw the ferry approaching. I still had about two kilometres to run, but the ferry always took at least ten minutes to unload and load its passengers, so I should have arrived there in plenty of time.

By now, I was thoroughly soaked and frozen to the very core of my being. Only the thought of that warm ferry kept me going. The pathway took me inland slightly, and I lost sight of the inbound boat. My next view of it was as I turned the final corner towards the dock. To my utter horror and disbelief, the ferry was reversing away from the pier. I had literally missed the boat. 'How the heck could this have happened?' I thought to myself between tears of frustration and hyperthermia. I knew that there were only two ferries a day at this time of the year, the one I had got to the island and the one that had just left. There was no way that I would be catching a boat from this dock today. And so, despite feeling like death, I turned around and headed back towards Centerville, hoping desperately that there would be a ferry there. If not, I had no idea what I was going to do. I had not thought this through properly!

Having already run over ten kilometres in the rain, hail, wind and snow, the prospect of another five kilometres filled me with dread. Unbelievably, the wind decided to change direction once again. I was again running into the teeth of a gale. As I made my way slowly towards the Centerville dock, I could see the ferry again approaching. I still had some way to go and began the pointless process of shouting into the storm. I did not have the energy to survive, missing another lift back towards the warmth and salvation of my hotel room. I put my head down and ran as fast as my frozen legs would allow. Thank goodness I made it literally by the skin of my teeth. Another minute and I would have been stranded on the island with a crew of eighteen and nearly four hundred passengers wondering where one their pilots were.

Mind you, if they knew what an idiot I had been attempting a run during weather like that, they would have probably wanted me to miss that ferry! If I thought that run was cold, I had obviously forgotten about Montreal and my trial by ice.

Montreal was not one of my regular destinations. It was usually served by the smaller Boeing 777. However, on the few times I visited, I made the most of my time there. My usual run would take me up Mont-Royal Park, a long, hard, twisting run to the summit. From here, there was a panoramic view across the city and onwards to the St Lawrence river. The run back down the hill took me towards the other side of the city for a gentle run back to the starting point. All in all, a pleasant way to spend the morning, well, most mornings. There was one extremely memorable day when things were very different.

We set off from London in very early January 1998. The forecast for Montreal was cold, with a fair chance of snow, especially the day after we arrived. Being naturally cautious about snow, we decided to take a lot of extra fuel in case the weather deteriorated earlier than expected. As it turned out, we landed in a clear, cold Montreal afternoon, nothing out of the ordinary considering the time of year. The following day, I donned my cold weather running gear, which basically meant I had a woolly hat and gloves to go with my shorts and tee shirt. Feeling very pleased with myself for taking these precautions, I set off to climb the park hill. It felt cold, really cold, as I set off but again, nothing that unusual, that was to come later.

Halfway up the hill, I noticed that the sky had started to change colour, and not in a good way. From my elevated vantage point, it looked as though night-time had decided to come early, even though it was barely ten o'clock in the morning. A tremendous black blanket was slowly eating up every bright corner of the sky. As this monster from above moved slowly towards me, some primaeval instinct told me that I should be anywhere except where I was at that precise moment. And so, for the first and last time in my running career, I turned and ran away from the weather. I ran just as fast as my legs could carry me. Sadly, they could not carry me fast enough.

I was still some way from the hotel when the storm first hit. All daylight was obliterated as it moved over me, and the day became night. The snow started in earnest a few moments later. By the time I reached safety, I resembled the abominable snowman. Still, I was back and back safely, which sadly, could not be said for everyone else in the city. Had I continued on up the hill, I very much doubt that I would have made it back safely, given the severity of the weather. Luckily, we managed to leave Montreal later on that day. The residents, however, had to endure days of misery as the full impact of that ice storm really hit. The crew who brought the aircraft we flew home on were stranded there for over a week as Montreal closed down and froze to a complete standstill.

I had made a very lucky escape that day and it turned out to be the very last time that I visited that city.

Chapter 22

Colourful, Exciting, and Dangerous

South America was not high up on my to-do list. The Boeing 747 was not utilised that often on the many exotic destinations on the continent. Whereas the Boeing 777 served such glamorous destinations as Rio De Janeiro and Bueno Aires, we went to São Paulo.

The city itself was one of the most crowded places on earth, with nearly twelve and a half million people crammed into a relatively small area. Brazil's industrial and commercial centre was more a place to work than play. 'Earn in São Paulo, spend in Rio' was a popular quotation. Whilst both cities can be dangerous, at least Rio had Copacabana, Sugarloaf mountain, and Corcovado; São Paulo had skyscrapers.

The first time I visited São Paulo was not an enjoyable experience for a number of reasons, which I am convinced clouded my judgement of the city.

I was sitting at home enjoying the 2015 Rugby World Cup. Rugby has always been my favourite sport; I played to a reasonable standard in the day. England were hosting the tournament, and I, along with most English supporters, had high hopes for England's chances of lifting the trophy. It was Thursday, 24th September and one of the biggest matches was due to take place that weekend, England were playing Wales. We were overwhelming favourites, and I only hoped that we did not humiliate the Welsh too much. I was on my annual standby month, but so certain was I that nobody would dare go sick on such an important weekend, I had invited a number of friends around to watch the match. And then the phone rang.

Two hours later, I was thumping my backside into the left-hand seat of my Boeing 747, trying not to appear too grumpy. I had two relatively young first officers. Both seemed very pleasant at first sight, and then they opened their mouths. They were both Welsh. Immediately, I felt very sorry for them, especially when they informed me that they had requested the trip together to watch the rugby in São Paulo. 'Fancy going all that way to watch your team being beaten', I thought to myself quietly. Well, I must have imagined that I said it quietly to myself as they both assured me that Wales had a good chance of winning. 'There goes their chance of doing a landing on this trip'. I made absolutely sure that this time I really did say it to myself.

It's a long way to São Paulo; nearly twelve hours, which is a long time if you didn't want to go there in the first place. It's even longer if you have to listen to two really keen Welsh rugby supporters. Landing into São Paulo was never straightforward. The language barrier and the sheer number of other aircraft made for a challenging environment. After getting to the hotel on Friday morning, I was more than ready for bed.

The next morning, I was up early. I wanted to complete my run in plenty of time to get back, shower and change. I had arranged to meet my new Welsh friends at a local pub that was showing the match. They had done all the hard work before leaving London. They had even booked a table near the television, I was slowly warming to both of them.

I had planned a route from the hotel down to the famous Interlargo racing track and back via a different route. The match was being shown live at lunchtime local time, so I made an early start.

For every destination we visited, the company would provide us with a briefing sheet for the city we were staying in. Normally, this described local customs, telephone numbers in case of emergencies and even places to visit or good local restaurants. The briefing sheet for São Paulo had a whole page dedicated to staying safe. In big, bold, capital letters, it strongly advised us not to go out alone. We were also advised not to take any valuables; no phones, watches, jewellery, or anything that could be the target of a thief. As this was my first time in the city, I thought I had better err on the safe side. Obviously, no one was daft enough to run with me, so going out in pairs was literally a non-starter.

Instead, I reluctantly took off my watch and my iPhone and placed them in the room safe. These were my only valuables, so I was confident that I was not going to be a target for any muggers. I drew a map of my route and played it smart by not leaving it on the table. Finally, I put my trusted twenty dollar note in my pocket as a last resort to appease any attacker. And with those preparations in place, I left the hotel in search of Interlagos. The run and, in fact, the whole day, didn't go as well as I had hoped.

Coming out of the hotel, I crossed a busy main road. This is not as easy as it sounds. Drivers in the city seemed to have two aims: drive as quickly as possible and run over anyone stupid enough to get in their way. It was one of those rare occasions where drivers seemed to swerve to hit rather than avoid pedestrians. Eventually, taking my life in my hands, I made it to the other side of the road. From there, I settled down to a reasonably good pace. I was starting to enjoy myself. I passed a few roads that looked inviting. A lot of the old city still remained between the numerous skyscrapers. It was into this warren of old and narrow streets that a very stupid and unprepared runner left the relative safety of the main streets.

Consulting my badly drawn map, eventually, I found the street that would, hopefully, take me towards my destination. Leaving the busy street, I should have realised that I had made a crucial error. Instead of a wide road, I was now in a labyrinth of small, narrow alleyways. The hairs on the back of my neck stood up as it began to dawn on me that this was not a good place to be in. I decided to turn around and head back towards the busy area I had just left.

I had gone but a few yards when two youths stepped out in front of me, completely blocking my way. Not wanting to confront these two rather unpleasant characters, I turned around and, to avoid any unpleasantness, I tried to run back the way I had come. As I turned, another two equally unpleasant characters stood immediately behind me. I was trapped in a very narrow alleyway, two in front, two behind. My morning was rapidly going downhill.

When confronted with impossible odds, there are three things you can do. The first is to panic and try to run away; the second is to try and fight your way out; the third is to appeal to your opponents.

I don't panic easily, I don't fight very often, so I chose the third option.

They demanded, in very good English, a fact I complimented them on, that I hand over all my valuables.

I was tempted to ask if they had read the British Airways station brief. If so, they would know that I had nothing of value on me, I was keeping my twenty dollars, literally in my back pocket for now.

I was now talking to the two individuals that had first stepped out in front of me. The really ugly one shouted in my face, "Money." I replied, "Thank you very much, but I have some."

This took him some moments to comprehend. His much better-looking and obviously brighter companion started to laugh. His partner in crime was obviously confused and said something very unpleasant to me, best not to repeat exactly what he said but my mother would have been very offended. He grabbed my running vest and again, demanded money. He was so angry that I did not think my twenty dollars was going to help me. His face was now inches from mine as he shouted and spat into my face. He wanted money or jewellery or both, and he wanted them now. I tried to resort to my one and only ace, a twenty dollar note. I held it up as a peace offering, giving this most unpleasant individual what I considered to be my most disarming and friendly smile. He snatched the money from my hand and threw it on the floor. At that point, I knew I was in serious trouble. If my money could not appease him, then my smile certainly wasn't going to. I only had one more trick up my sleeve; if that didn't work, I was not going to make the match or anything else.

Standing in front of my two assailants, I pointed out that I was in my running gear. I had nothing else on me. I pulled out my pockets, empty. I pointed to my wrists, nothing there. I pointed to my old running vest and equally old pair of shorts. If I was rich, would I be wearing clothes such as these I asked them? And then it was all or nothing, and I played my last card.

I pointed to my very old running shoes. Luckily, I had not replaced them yet. I demanded that they look at my shoes and then look at theirs. They both wore very new and very fashionable trainers. "Who should be mugging who?" I asked as politely as I could.

This tactic had worked for me the previous time I had tried it. I just hoped it worked again. Try standing in front of someone and pointing to your shoes at the same time as asking them to look. Their eyes will almost involuntarily follow where you are pointing. It will only be for a microsecond, but it will give you a chance to catch them off guard. It worked. They both glanced at my feet.

Suddenly, I was eighteen years old, back on the rugby pitch. In front of me were two opposition players intent on bringing me to the ground. Behind were two more players trying to catch me. Four to one, I had beaten those odds before, and as if my life depended on it, which, to be fair, it probably did now, I made my play.

My left hand shot out into the face of the most vicious-looking mugger, just as it would have if I had handed off an opponent. I heard a crunching noise as my palm made contact with his nose. I consoled myself with the thought that he could not get any uglier. Then, I put my right shoulder into the other assailant in front of me, and he staggered sideways. I ran between them and set off as quickly as my trembling legs could carry me.

The alleyway was narrow and deserted. I could hear the sounds of my now really angry muggers as they gave chase. I dared not look around, but I guessed that the two people behind me had struggled to get past their fallen friends. They were in their twenties, and I was in my fifties. I didn't hold out a great deal of hope. Suddenly, I remembered that I was eighteen again and about to score a spectacular try. I found some extra pace, and the sounds of their footsteps faded slightly.

Next, I burst out onto a really busy shopping street. I still dared not look back. Instead, I dodged between the shoppers, ran across the busy road and into a shopping mall.

I received some very strange looks from a pair of security guards as I tried to catch my breath. I approached them and pointed to my map and my hotel's name. My Portuguese was about as good as their English, but eventually, one of them took my little map and drew a route back to the hotel. Thirty minutes later, I opened the door to my room, quickly checking that I had not been followed, and shut the door behind me. It took me a while to recover my composure. That had probably been the closest I had ever come to having something sharp inserted between my ribs. Shuddering at the thought, I had a quick shower; the real rugby match was kicking off in less than an hour.

Eventually, I found the Irish pub where my first officers had booked a table. Only the Irish could have opened a pub in such a place. I walked into the overcrowded bar and was astounded at what greeted me. There was a wall of red shirts, all proudly displaying the Welsh Dragon. It was like I had been transported to the Principality Stadium in Cardiff. 'Where the hell have all these Welshmen appeared from?' That was my first thought. As I made my way to the front, my second thought was that I was glad that I was not wearing my England shirt. Luckily, I packed in such a hurry that I had left it at home. Everyone just accepted that I was Welsh. I had my fill of conflict for one day, so I did not correct anyone when they slapped my back and assured me that we would beat the dreaded English.

I found my workmates seated at their table with about ten beers each in front of them. There was an empty seat with another ten beers in front of it. As I settled down to watch the Welsh being demolished, I tucked into my beers. I felt a wave of sympathy for all these red-shirted supporters. In eighty minutes, they would be devastated as their team was knocked out of the World Cup.

Instead, it was me that was devastated. England lost by three points. Whilst everyone around me went berserk, I noticed a sad, lonely figure sitting by himself. Bravely, he was wearing an England shirt. I went over to join him. I sat down. He looked up at me with a tear in his eye.

"I used to play rugby with Bob Hiller," was his opening remark. Luckily, I was old enough to remember that Bob Hiller was the England captain in the early 1970s.

"I used a rugby handoff and a shoulder charge to fend off two assailants this morning," was the only reply that came to mind. He was probably as equally confused by my remark as I was by his. We lapsed back into silence, looking at the beers in front of us.

I asked him if he fancied another beer.

"But we lost," was his immediate reply.

"Yep, but we are both still alive," I reassured him as I left to fight my way to the bar.

For me, it was not a happy flight back to London the next evening. Twelve hours of being reminded about Gareth Davies's last-minute try did nothing to brighten my mood. It was a long time before I returned to São Paulo, and then again, it was because some wise captain had decided to go sick.

Chapter 23

A Champion at Last!

Cairo is the city of the Pyramids, one of the Seven Wonders of the World. The city contrasts incredible beauty with great danger. Despite a relatively short flight time of five and a half hours, we were lucky enough to have a night stop in this mysterious city. The approach was always fun. I would ask for a slight detour to the right on every approach due to the weather. The fact that there was no weather and the detour took me directly over the pyramids luckily seemed to escape the tower controller.

Due to ongoing security concerns, we were accommodated in a large hotel complex on its own grounds outside the city. The hotel was protected by armed security, with guards patrolling twenty-four hours a day. We were safe inside this complex, so what did I do? Well, of course, I prepared an escape plan. Initially, I tried my well-used and trusted method of running to the security post and asking to be allowed out for a run. This usually worked, although only sometimes to my advantage, as has already been demonstrated. This time, however, it was very different. As I approached the security post, two heavily armed guards emerged from their hut, weapons raised. It is always best not to argue with anyone with a gun pointed at you. I could see no reason to change this philosophy, so I turned around and ran quickly back towards the hotel.

At this point, I noticed a large brick wall on one side of the path. I was now out of view from the security post, so I quickly looked to see what was on the other side of the wall. By now, you would have thought I'd have learnt my lesson and returned to my room meekly. If I had done that, I would never have become a champion. Although I'm still trying to figure out what I am a champion of, I am a true champion of something.

The wall was tall, well over ten feet high. Luckily for me, the wall was not in the best state of repair, and I managed to find enough foot and hand holes to scale it easily. Sitting astride the top, I could not quite believe what I saw. There, in front of me, was a vast park with a horse racing circuit around the perimeter, complete with stables at one side. Further inside the track were several football pitches complete with teams eagerly enjoying their matches. 'Well, what a splendid place to run', I thought to myself. 'What harm could I come to in such an idyllic place?' With that thought firmly at the front of my mind, I slid down the other side of the wall and despite landing awkwardly, I set off towards the horse racing track.

As I got closer to the grandstand, I could see that, luckily, there were no horse racing events on today. I ducked beneath the white post and rail fencing and joined the track. 'Three laps of the circuit should be sufficient,' I thought to myself, as I rounded the tight corner that brought me out in front of the grandstand. Imagine my horror and embarrassment as I suddenly realised that the stands were not empty at all and that a race was about to begin.

Fortunately for me, today's race was for humans, not horses. A pack of about twenty runners set off just as I approached from the rear. 'What do I do now?' I thought to myself. Strangely, 'keep going,' was the answer I came up with. And so I did. I kept running and followed the pack. Their pace confused me, as quickly, I caught up and passed those at the rear of the group. Nobody seemed to notice me. I have always had a slight, tanned Mediterranean look about me, so I assumed they mistook me for a local. Anyway, nobody rugby tackled me and dragged me away. We were now halfway down the straight and approaching the first corner. I had managed to catch the front runners and was now competing for the lead. I am not the fastest runner in the world, and I struggled to understand why my fellow runners were going so slowly. And then it suddenly dawned on me they were probably running a half or even full marathon. I was happy with a ten-kilometre run. No wonder they were conserving their energy.

To avoid any further embarrassment, I decided to kick on and leave them to their race whilst I ran mine. By this time, we were on the back straight of the course. I guessed that the circuit was about four or five kilometres in length. Three other runners came with me as I tried to pull away from the pack. Now, this really was embarrassing. I was ruining their race, forcing them to go faster than they needed to. However, I had made my choice to run ahead, and it seemed wrong now to slow down.

As we came around the last corner, true to form, I had decided not to allow them to pass me, and so the four of us began to race in earnest. If they kept this pace up for the rest of their marathon, a few records would be broken. I was still in the lead as we came abreast of the stands once more, only another hundred metres from the point where we had started. To my amazement, two officials strung a tape across the track; moments later, I broke it as I ran past the officials.

I had won a race! Not only had I won it, but I had also won it well. The other runners were only just finishing. I stopped and looked back. People were pointing at me and waving their hands. It was definitely a good time to leave, not a good time to go back and claim my prize. I ran behind the stand and sprinted to the wall I had transversed earlier. Up and over I went in record time, landing flat on my backside in my haste to make a quick exit.

I still wonder what those runners, spectators and officials thought of the phantom runner. Sadly, I will never know what I won, but possibly it was the slowest run ever held in front of that Cairo grandstand.

Over the years, I ran that same course many times. Despite all the warnings about security, I never once encountered anything even slightly approaching aggression. Indeed, it was the opposite. Everyone was friendly and welcoming. I was invited into the stables to meet the racehorses on one occasion. The trainer had seen me struggling to climb over the wall and asked if I needed a hand. I assured him I was actually an Egyptian champion and needed no help. Despite my protestations, he still gave me a leg up. Bless him.

I went back to Cairo six months later. I set off for my normal run. Three minutes later, I stood in front of the wall that was my gateway to the racetrack. I looked in despair as the new and fortified barrier was not one I could transverse. Gone was the old wall. Barbed wire and an electrified deterrent now stood in my way. Well, there was no way even I was going over that. Sadly, I turned around and walked back to my room. My running affair with Cairo was at an end. When the Boeing 777 took over the route a few weeks later, I was not that upset.

Chapter 24

Lost in the Land of the Rising Sun

Japan was another strange place to go for a run and for no other reason than nobody spoke English. The road signs were totally unreadable unless you had a good handle on the language. In my experience, Japan was unique in this respect. It was the only country I have visited where I felt totally alien, a complete stranger. Going into a shop, I had absolutely no idea what was being sold. This mainly applied to food stores. Being a vegetarian was impossible as far as I could see, as everything had the face of a fish or animal on it. This was in complete contrast to China, where the roads had an English translation. In cities such as Beijing, all the restaurants also had a menu in English.

Usually, we stayed just outside Tokyo in Narita. Airline crews from all over the world descended upon Narita for their stopovers. As it was so difficult to know where to eat and drink, all international crews tended to conjugate in the same few places that catered for these foreign visitors. The cost was also a problem for visiting crews. The price of a beer was eye-watering compared to most other countries. A local entrepreneur soon solved this problem by parking a massive articulated lorry in the hotel car park. He had converted the interior into a bar, complete with everything you could need, toilets included. He charged less than half the price of the local bars, and the legend of 'The Truck' was born. Who else but airline crews would fly halfway around the world to spend their evenings in the back of a lorry?

For my first run in Japan, long before smart or even mobile phones, I decided to run from the hotel to what looked like a fascinating local landmark, the Naritasan Shinshoji Temple. It looked interesting. I have no idea what it was like as I never found it!

Full of what turned out to be a hopelessly overly optimistic faith in my map reading abilities, I set off from the hotel. The infamous truck was my first point of reference, situated diagonally across the huge car park which serviced three other giant hotels. Sadly, I had succumbed to the irresistible charms of this establishment the previous evening, and I was not feeling my best as I set off on my run. Still, I consoled myself with the thought that running had always proved to be the perfect cure for a hangover. Surely my headache would soon disappear. In the daylight, I noticed for the first time, a deep ravine between my hotel and the truck. I stopped and looked around me. 'How do I get across this?' I wondered. It then occurred to me that I had already made this journey twice in complete darkness just the previous evening. I looked around, trying to resolve this conundrum. Suddenly, I noticed a narrow walkway to my right. Somehow we had managed to cross the ravine twice, the second time a little more unsteadily than the first, without even knowing it was there. I found out later that day that others had not been so fortunate. A few had ended up at the bottom of the ditch with various injuries. A little while after this incident, the owner of the truck felt compelled to provide lights to guide his customers away from disaster. Apparently, he was losing too many inebriated customers to broken bones.

With this first obstacle successfully navigated, I referred to my map and headed for what I thought would be the road to the temple. Well, it looked about right. What could possibly go wrong?

Thirty minutes later, my question was answered. Everything that could go wrong had indeed gone wrong. I kept persuading myself that the road, or path I was running on, coincided with the one I was looking at on the map. Finally, I had to admit to myself that the rice field I was standing in, with the water just below my knees, was definitely not the public park I was aiming for. I was sure that Naritasan Park had much more to offer than rows of rice plants harvested by old ladies in straw hats. These lovely ladies looked equally as confused as I was. They had probably never seen a European man standing in their paddy fields scratching his head and looking at what was now a very soggy map. To add to my problems, it was now pouring down with rain.

I gave up my temple visit plan and decided to return to the hotel. I was now very wet and freezing, a state, unfortunately, I found myself in far more often than not on my runs. My hangover had also decided to accompany me this far and showed no signs of wanting to leave. And so, we both turned around and set off back in the direction of the truck, a place where all my problems had started the previous evening. If I thought I had problems now, boy, was I in for a shock. My problems were only just beginning.

I had entered the paddy field from a narrow track and had run, well-splashed, diagonally across the vast fields. There was no focal point to get my bearings, just a huge expanse of rice fields - no trees, no bushes, no fences or walls, just rice. I looked at what was left of my map. It showed roads and parks but stubbornly refused to show any paddy fields. It dawned on me that I had run off my map. I was literally off-grid. 'Oh well, I will retrace my steps back the way I had just come', I thought to myself.

That worked very well right up to the moment I could not find the point where I had entered the rice field. I was so busy running and trying to look at my map, I had completely forgotten to take note of where I had entered this waterlogged landscape. At this point, I wanted to burst into tears. I craved to find myself warm and dry in my hotel room, gently nursing my hangover.

I looked around for the rice pickers. Maybe, they could help? Forgetting that almost nobody here could speak a word of English, least of all these elderly ladies, I still decided to seek out their help. The only problem was they had all disappeared, probably to inform the authorities of the mad foreigner trampling their crop. With few other choices, I picked a path that looked like a likely candidate to lead me back to the truck and my hotel. I set off once again. I felt very sorry for myself, but I had to keep moving or be in real trouble. Fifteen minutes later, I found myself standing next to a busy road. 'This was progress', I thought to myself until I realised that all the signs were in Japanese.

There were not even little pictures to give me a clue as to where I was. I felt utterly helpless. For the first time, I felt that I was in a completely and utterly foreign land. I had no idea what to do. Nothing looked familiar. Everything was strange and totally alien to what I was used to. I had no idea where I was or which way I needed to go. What made it even worse was that I had no way of asking anyone the way back to the hotel. It made little difference anyway, as there was nobody about. Anyway, I had even forgotten the name of the hotel I was staying at. I sat on a wet bench and felt a wave of complete hopelessness wash over me. I was totally alone in a very foreign land with no company, apart from my hangover, which was proving to be a very loyal and persistent companion. It was obviously going to stay with me through thick and thin. We had bonded; we were a team.

The only thing I could do was run along this road until I either came to a police station or another hotel. My rationale was that my hotel receptionist had spoken English. If I could get to any hotel, I could plead my case and be understood. Hopefully, they could also check which hotel British Airways crews stayed in. It was quite a pathetic plan, but it was the only one I could think of. With that, I checked if my hangover was ready to go. Apparently, it was, so we both set off, hopefully, in the direction of the nearest hotel.

Just when I thought that the weather could not get any worse, it did. The rain was bouncing back off the pavement and meeting the rain coming down in the opposite direction. The traffic was racing along the road, which was quickly becoming a river. The locals obviously did not slow down for a mere deluge. Car after car threw spray all over me, adding to my total and absolute misery. Half an hour later, I spotted what I hoped was a hotel. It wasn't easy to tell at first due to the minimal visibility. However, as I got closer, the very welcoming neon sign, proclaiming the building to be a Hilton, shone through the gloom. For the first time since finding myself in a paddy field, my spirits rose, and I accelerated towards the sanctuary of the reception area.

As I entered the warmth of the lobby, I only just managed to resist shaking myself like a wet dog. Instead, I did my best to brush away as much excess rain as possible before leaving a trail of water as I made my way to the reception desk. I stood in my running shorts and vest, trying to look as inconspicuous as possible. It was late autumn, and everyone else wore the appropriate clothing, so my efforts to blend in were in vain.

The hotel was busy, so I stood in line in front of one of the receptionists, the puddle beneath me gradually expanding across the marble floor. At least, this gave me more space as other guests moved away to avoid the excess water, or maybe it was me they wanted to avoid. Eventually, it was my turn. Now usually, it is relatively easy to make yourself understood when checking into a hotel. A simple "do you have a room, please?" followed by the offering of a room key and a smile is usually the conversation's extent.

Instead, I asked if she knew which hotel the British Airways crew stayed in. This totally threw her. She spoke English, but only to the extent of phrases you used in hotels. She was by no means fluent. I was not fluent in her language. Indeed, I did not even know one word of Japanese.

After repeating my question three times, she finally confirmed that the British Airways crew did not stay at this hotel. Now, although I needed to know which hotel I was staying in, I knew which ones I was not staying in, so this little gem of information did not help me that much. I tried again, and she once again confirmed that there were no British Airways crew at the Hilton. She started to look over my shoulder to beckon the next guest forward and get rid of this soaking-wet and inappropriately dressed foreigner.

I would not be dismissed so easily in this fashion. I moved sideways to prevent the person behind me from taking my place at the head of the queue. I asked her if there was anyone else could help me acquire the information I so desperately needed. With an obviously annoyed attitude, she stood up and disappeared into a back room behind the reception desk. A few moments later, she reappeared with a small piece of paper and threw it at me. With that, I was dismissed, and the next guest pushed past me to be served. Everyone was obviously pleased to see the back of me.

The name of a hotel I vaguely recognised was on the piece of paper. I walked to the concierge desk and handed over my little bit of paper. He looked at me, looked again, and then said just one word, "Taxi?" I had no money on me or in my room. I had spent it all the previous night. I made a walking sign using two fingers and received a very quizzical look in response. He informed me that the weather was not very good for walking. I thought the state of me would have given him a clue that I was aware of the conditions outside. He then very kindly drew me a little map of how to get to my hotel.

For the second time that day, I left a nice, warm, dry hotel with a little map, hoping to get to my destination. Twenty minutes later, I entered the car park I had left earlier that day. The rain had now disappeared, and my hangover had decided to follow it. Shortly afterwards, I lay in a very hot bath, trying to recover from my little adventure. I tried desperately to see the funny side before deciding that there wasn't one.

I met up with the crew later that night as previously arranged. To my dismay, we headed once again for the notorious truck. Two hours and a lot of beer and nibbles later, I had had enough. I was tired and a little the worse for wear. The rest of the crew were going to make a night of it, so I bade them goodnight and set off alone to return to the hotel. Five minutes later, I found myself at the bottom of the creek I had somehow managed to avoid the previous night. It was not a good end to an already horrible day.

Chapter 25

It's a Small World

One of my favourite routes on the Boeing 747 was the longest flight we did, London to Singapore, a couple of days rest, then onwards to Sydney or Melbourne. It isn't easy to believe that we were only given one day's rest in Australia before flying home. Believe me, it's a very long way to go for twenty-four hours of rest. For a short period, some bright spark in flight planning had espoused the brilliant idea that two pilots could fly from Singapore to Melbourne. Landing at six in the morning, they would then be flying back to Singapore that afternoon. In other words, fly to Australia, spend twelve hours in the country and fly home again. Although it was just legal, it was immoral. It was also dangerous. I would love to have seen the manager who approved this exhausting sector try to fly that schedule. Luckily, if we were more than thirty minutes late on arrival, the pilots would run out of duty hours unless the captain specifically approved an extension and only a few ever did. I was never one who extended the duty hours. After a couple of months, the experiment was abandoned, and the manager was promoted to something more appropriate to his abilities, hopefully, something like ordering paper clips.

Running in Singapore changed dramatically over the decades. When I first visited in the late 1980s, Singapore managed to show signs of its colonial past. Still standing, there were a few old-style houses and hotels, the most famous of which was the world-renowned Raffles Hotel. As a crew, we were lucky enough to stay at that beautiful hotel decades later. When I first visited Singapore, we stayed at the now-defunct Marco Polo Hotel. As with most of the Singapore I first knew, this building has now been knocked down to make way for bright, new, shiny offices and apartments. This hotel was close to a park with lovely tracks to run along, which has long since been bulldozed and redeveloped. After a sweaty and humid five kilometres on this particular day, I collapsed onto a sun bed and fell fast asleep. Over an hour later, having lain on my side for the majority of the time, I woke up to a stinging sensation down one side of my face and body. Thinking I had caught some dreadful disease, I rushed back to my room to investigate further.

Looking into my bathroom mirror, I was horrified at the vision staring back at me. I had not been in the sunshine for several months. Well, one side of my body had not been. The other half was now a bright and painful red. I looked like a steak that had only been cooked on one side. The most embarrassing thing was that my face had suffered the same fate. I looked ridiculous. This was 1987, and I was still undergoing line training with a particularly fussy training captain. When I reported for duty the next day, the look on his face said it all. I was sternly informed that this type of stupidity was not expected of new first officers. His parting comment was for me to keep out of sight and not scare any passengers.

This was a ten-day trip, and on each subsequent day, my sunburnt appearance got worse. The red turned to a deeper shade, with the occasional blister erupting around one side of my burnt face. A few days later, my skin gave up trying to stay on my face and began to peel off in large strips. Now, I looked like I had scurvy and the captain refused to let me leave the flight deck on our return journey. My training file for that trip contained words and phrases such as 'idiot ', foolish', and 'should know better'. Reluctantly, I had to admit that they were largely fair and well-deserved comments.

My runs in Singapore were interesting mainly because, especially in the early years, I seemed to be the only person out running. The heat and humidity can be fierce at certain times of the year; it's never actually cool, but occasionally the weather drains every ounce of energy out of you. I kept my running to a maximum of five kilometres. Even then, I would sometimes return feeling slightly unwell.

By this time, we had moved to stay in the city's heart, making running slightly more complicated. I still set off every morning, running along the busy streets. One of my favourite places was Bugis Street, where you could still find something of the old Singapore along the busy market stalls. In October each year, these streets that I had got to know so well were closed for the Singapore Grand Prix. I was lucky enough to have a room with a balcony and watched in awe as the cars weaved around these narrow streets. I found it difficult enough at twelve kilometres an hour. These guys were doing it at over three hundred kilometres an hour! And next for me, I was onward bound, off to Australia.

By the time I was senior enough to get the very sought-after Australian flights, there were, sadly, only two destinations we flew to: Sydney and Melbourne. Today, only Sydney is served by British Airways. When mentioning Australia, people tend to think of Sydney, the Opera House and the Harbour Bridge. However, Melbourne is also a wonderful city and quickly became one of my favourite places to run. Time was always a problem when considering my run down under. We had a maximum of twenty-four hours in the country, sometimes as little as twelve hours. Considering we had flown all the way from the UK via Singapore, the body clock was a little confused, to say the least. After landing, going through the endless Australian immigration procedures and getting the bus to the hotel, there was very little time for anything else but sleep unless you made the time, which of course, I did.

Even I had to admit that on the twelve-hour layover, with the minimal time we had in the hotel, around eight hours, there was little time for anything but sleep. However, I always made time for a quick thirty-minute run before the bus picked us up for the return flight. Luckily, most of my visits were the twenty-four-hour layovers, so there was plenty of time to get out and about. Our hotel was in downtown Melbourne on the south bank of the river Yarra. The location was perfect; I would be running along the river on the Yarra Trail five minutes after leaving the hotel. This would take me towards Alexandra Gardens and beyond. Being in the city's heart, running along a purpose-made track, always made me smile and lifted my spirits. Reaching the park made it hard to believe I was still in the city. Rolling green spaces stretched toward the river. Here, families were picnicking and enjoying the weather.

A little further along, I was running between the rowing clubhouses and the waterside. It was like a scene from the Oxford and Cambridge annual boat race. It wasn't easy to believe that I was not running alongside the river Thames. On one memorable occasion, I was stopped by a group of seven rowers looking sadly, at an eight-man boat. There was, of course, one spare seat. Had I ever rowed, was their first question? I readily admitted that I was once a rowing club member, and yes, I had rowed in a very similar boat to the one sitting at their feet. Predictably, the next question was, did I fancy making up their numbers? They had been let down at the last minute. This was so Australian. I loved their attitude to all things sport - get out there and do it. Did I fancy making up the numbers? Of course I did, and I felt my heart rate start to race at the prospect of rowing again.

Sadly, it never happened. Having agreed to row and starting to put on the team shirt, the errant rower made a very belated arrival. However, half the team still wanted me to row with them. Apparently, this individual made a habit of arriving late or not arriving at all. He needed to be taught a lesson. Sanity prevailed when the club captain came over to preside on the matter at hand. I watched with mounting jealousy as they raced down the river. In retrospect, it was a good thing, as I had failed to mention that it was over twenty years since I had last pulled an oar. I would almost certainly have made a fool of myself. Still, how often does a British pilot get asked to row for a team in Australia? I consoled myself with this thought as I chased after their boat. I could, at least, race them along the riverbank if I could not row with them. Quite soon, I lost sight of the boat as they easily outpaced me. Still, it was another first on one of my runs, and the disappointment soon wore off as I made my way towards the Botanical Gardens.

My usual route took me along the river; depending on how jetlagged I felt, I would cross the river after passing the fourth or fifth bridge. Time then, for the equally spectacular return leg. This time, I was running towards Melbourne Park and the home of the Australian Tennis Open. I have been lucky enough to have visited Wimbledon and have seen Flushing Meadows in New York. However, the setting of the Rod Laver Arena and the rest of the Australian Tennis Centre does set it apart. It is spectacular. The whole complex nestles beside the river, giving it a serene appearance. I was always surprised at how close I was allowed to run to those show courts, even when the Australian Open was on. If I had tried that at Wimbledon, I would have been led away to a waiting police car.

One hot sunny afternoon, I was making my way towards the tennis courts. As usual, I was in my own world, thinking about how good that first ice-cold beer would taste in an hour's time. Suddenly, I thought I heard someone call out my name. I knew the crew would probably still be asleep, and I didn't know anyone in Melbourne. I kept on running. The next thing I heard was, "Nick, you silly bugger, stop," which of course I did. There behind me, panting away at the effort of turning around and chasing me, was a school friend I had last seen over thirty-five years ago. I could hardly believe the sheer coincidence of him emigrating to Melbourne and choosing that exact time to go for the same run as I had! We stood there reminiscing about the good old days. He came up with names I had not heard or thought about for decades. He seemed to remember everyone.

I had to be very careful as my memory for faces is excellent; sadly, my memory for names could be better. I managed to get through the whole conversation without me having to mention his name. Eventually, as we parted with promises to keep in touch, I breathed a sigh of relief. To this very day, I have absolutely no idea of his name. If he ever reads this, then I apologise profusely. Even looking in the mirror, sometimes, I can place the face looking back at me, but I struggle with the name. Despite swapping mobile numbers, we never spoke again. Or maybe, he did call, but as I did not recognise the name, I probably deleted the message.

A little further north, Sydney also had a spectacular landscape. In fact, it had some of the most iconic landmarks in the world. The best way to see these sights was to strap on a pair of running shoes and set off.

The most challenging decision I had to make on that very first run was what to see first. The Opera House was obviously very high on my list, as was Sydney Harbour Bridge. The Botanical Gardens and the Rocks were also on my to-see list.

Being totally unable to make up my mind, a little like a young child let loose in a sweet shop, I decided I wanted to visit them all on the same run. It was a very ambitious plan, in truth, too ambitious for the time I had available.

As I set off mid-morning, there was no way of knowing that this run would get the better of me. Our hotel was situated in the Haymarket area of downtown Sydney, ideally located in the centre of the city. It was a hot day, although not hot enough to bother me unduly. It would have been good to check the weather forecast before I set off, hindsight being a wonderful thing.

The first part of the run went very well. Leaving the hotel, I set off down George Street, heading towards the harbour and the famous Rocks area. This was my first time in Sydney, and as I made my way down the busy street, I was unprepared for the incredible views that were about to greet me. Suddenly, the Harbour Bridge materialised from behind a tall office building. From here, my run was going to take me through the Rocks, with its pavement bars and restaurants and onto the bridge itself. It was now getting towards midday, and although I had been running for only twenty minutes, I was beginning to feel the effects of the heat. I noticed that people were starting to wait at the numerous public water fountains. I considered joining the queues, but that would waste time, so on I went.

Running across the bridge was one of those iconic moments that runners, or anyone, could never forget. Halfway across, I had to stop and take in the scenery in front, to either side and behind me. All thoughts of the excessive heat were forgotten as I stared at the Opera House and Botanical Gardens. My pace picked up, and quickly. I completed the crossing of the bridge which I intended to recross after a short run of Bradfield Park. However, the increasing temperature persuaded me to abandon this part of the run. Instead, I turned around and retraced my steps across the bridge. I ran back through the Rocks, noticing that the length of the queues for the drinking fountains had grown even longer. 'Oh well, I don't really need a drink', I thought to myself. I never carried my own supply, so I was used to being thirsty on a run.

All thoughts of water were forgotten as I approached the Sydney Opera House. The scale of the building was difficult to comprehend until you got up close and personal. It was far more extensive and more impressive than I had imagined. One of my mantras when running was never to stop until the run was completed. On this occasion, I stopped for the second time as I took in the scene in front of me. I promised myself that one day I would return to enjoy a performance in this building, a promise I have yet to keep.

I had now been running for about an hour as I headed away from the Opera House and towards the Botanical Gardens. This vast park is the perfect place in which to run. Initially, I followed the waterside path, once again, enjoying the panoramic views across the harbour. I checked my watch. I had now been running for nearly ninety minutes. The crew bus was due to pick us up from the hotel at four o'clock, in just over two hours' time. It was time to turn back. I left the harbour path to run through the gardens and onwards to the hotel, a distance of around five kilometres. A quick calculation had me back at the hotel about an hour before pick-up, a little tight but still comfortable. The day's heat was getting progressively worse, and I kept running in the shade as much as possible. My pace had noticeably slowed, and I headed for a drinking water fountain which I could see across a large open area of grass. Leaving the path, I ran diagonally across this grassland. By now, I really, really, needed a drink.

Halfway across this expanse of grass, I felt an excruciating pain in my right calf muscle. I went down head-first into the long grass. My immediate thought was that I had been bitten by a snake. Signs along the walkways warned of the dangers of straying off the paths. I started to panic. If the snake had bitten me on my calf, he was probably coming to finish what he had started. I looked down at my calf, which felt like it was about to part company with the lower part of my leg but there was no time to stop and have a closer look. I needed to get to a place of safety as quickly as I could. In great pain, I hopped across the remainder of the grassland and only stopped once I was safely back on the path.

Collapsing on an empty bench, I examined my calf, looking for the tell-tale pinprick holes confirming a snake bite. After a few minutes, I decided that I had not, after all, been bitten. Yet my calf had become rock hard and still hurt quite a lot. Aware that time was fast becoming an issue, I tried to stand up and put some weight on my damaged leg. The pain confirmed something was seriously wrong, so I sat down again. I gently began to massage my calf to relieve the pain and reduce the stiffness. After ten minutes of gentle massage, I noticed deep bruising started to develop at the back of my calf. I realised that I had torn or ruptured my calf muscle. Looking at my watch, I realised that the crew would soon be getting their wake-up calls for the flight back to Singapore. Instead of being in bed like them, I was five kilometres from the hotel with a torn calf muscle. I had no way to get back to the hotel other than walking. Stupidly, I had not taken my usual twenty dollars of insurance money. In a few hours, there would be a Boeing 747 with nearly four hundred people sitting and waiting for a captain to fly them home.

I stood up and tried to put some weight on my leg. The massage had helped, although it still hurt. I could manage a strange half-walk, half-hopping movement. Decision made, I started on my way back to the hotel. It took me the best part of an hour and numerous bouts of mumbled swearing. My heart sank as I rounded the last corner, only to see my crew climbing onto the bus. The first officer ran over to me; he could still run, which was more than I could do. He began asking me where I had been. He was about to call the company to report me missing in action. Luckily, I had returned just in time.

After a quick discussion, we agreed that he should go ahead with the rest of the crew and I would hop, literally hop, in a taxi and see him on the aircraft. Getting to my room, I was distressed that, as usual, a phantom gorilla had somehow got into my room whilst I was out. He had thrown every single item of my clothing all over the room. He had emptied my wash bag and left my uniform on the floor. This often happened to me. Usually, I had an hour to clear up his mess, but today, I only had a few minutes. Five minutes later, I hobbled across the reception area and asked the concierge to call me a taxi. As he went to make the call, there was a tap on my shoulder. Turning around, the first officer and the rest of the crew stood behind me.

As I started to protest that they should be halfway to the airport, I was given a helping hand to the bus. Apparently, they had a vote and unanimously, decided to wait for me. I was deeply touched but still gave them all a good telling-off for not obeying me in the first place. The smile on my face gave away my true feelings, as nobody seemed too concerned at my reprimand. I managed to walk painfully, but luckily, without a noticeable limp, through the airport and onto the flight deck. We decided that the first officer was best placed to fly us back to Singapore. We pushed back five minutes early despite the late arrival at the airport. As the aircraft climbed into the night sky, I realised that running and myself would have to become strangers for the next few months, at least. Sadly, the injury took a little longer than a few months to heal completely. The doctors advised a good six months of recovery before starting to run again. True to form, I gave it six weeks, which is why it probably took far longer to heal than it should have done.

An interesting footnote is when I asked the doctor what could have caused the injury. He replied that running long distances in extreme heat, having no hydration, and being middle-aged probably had something to do with it. I explained when and where the injury occurred. Also, I mentioned that on landing in Singapore, the news channels were full of stories that

Sydney had experienced record-breaking high temperatures the previous day, and many people had been treated for heat exhaustion. That would explain all those long queues at the water fountains then.

Chapter 26

A Greek Odyssey

Greece has always been very high on my list of favourite destinations in Europe. The fact that my sister-in-law, Sally, has lived there for over thirty years and we loved visiting her and her lovely family probably had something to do with why I adored the place so much. We have been visiting Zakynthos regularly from the days when our children were babies right up to the present day. Despite being lucky enough to have enjoyed running in numerous different countries, one of my all-time favourite runs is in Zakynthos, on a route that took me from the small seaside resort of Kalamaki towards the island's airport and finally up a steep hill to pick up the main Zante road back towards the sea.

Leaving Sally's house, the run took me along a narrow winding road. Her house was situated very close to the island's airport. The runway passed the end of her garden which always gave an opportunity to wave to the family on their veranda as we arrived or left. This was not a long run, only eight kilometres, but with the normally high temperatures and the steep hill, it was always a challenging and fun run of which I've never got bored, even after so many years. The lane eventually led to the main road, and I would now have to be very careful to avoid the manic driving of the tourist buses and taxis. They ignored all road regulations as they hurtled around the local hotels dropping and picking up the tourists at an alarming rate. If you got in their way, God help you. They must have been on pay-by-passenger contract; I can think of no other reason for them to drive so recklessly, except perhaps it's simply the Greek ethos.

At this point, many years ago, I met a horse running in the opposite direction He was completely alone, running in the middle of the roads with cars and buses swerving around him. 'This was not going to end well', I thought to myself, as I turned around and ran after the horse. Luckily, he was so spooked by the whole experience that he had slowed to a trot, allowing me to catch up with him. Now, I am not by any means an equestrian type of chap. For me, horses are things you bet on, not sit on. So there was no way I was going to ride this animal. I managed to grab hold of its lead, or halter, or rein, or whatever the thing that hangs from its head is called. I had no idea what to do. Fortunately for both of us, the horse seemed to like the idea that someone had come to its aid, and immediately, it quietened down and walked calmly by my side. We were on a stretch of the road where there were no houses, just a petrol station about half a mile away. Even I know enough about horses to know that they don't need filling up with that kind of fuel. However, it was my best bet for getting help. Fifteen minutes later, I walked onto the forecourt, calmly followed by my new best friend. The motorists, filling their cars, just stood and stared at me. I tried my best to think of a funny remark about horsepower. Sadly, the only thing I could come up with was the line, 'a tiger in your tank', the catchphrase from an old television advert from the 1970s. I realised that no one had ever seen the commercial, and it had no relevance to my standing on a petrol forecourt with a horse in tow. So I just shut up.

A moment later, an attendant strode out from his office and marched towards me. 'This is going to be difficult to explain in my non-existent Greek', I thought to myself, as he bore down on me. Instead of being ordered off his property, he held out a hand to take the horse's lead; I mean rein. Smiling, he thanked me for returning his horse. Apparently, he often escaped from the field behind the garage. With that, he led the creature back from whence it had come. I turned around and continued my run, thinking to myself that one day, I should write a book about all the strange things that happened when I was out running. But quickly, I dismissed the idea. Well, I did for a decade or two.

Back on the road again, I retraced my steps before I turned off and started the steep climb up the hill. This was a hard slog, and I had to put my head down and kick hard to avoid coming to a grinding halt. The effort was worth it though, as the views from the top were fabulous. I looked back behind, and the airport sat below me. It felt more like flying into the airport than running beside it. Ahead of me, I could see the half-collapsed mountain that stood majestically above the capital, Zante Town. The hill split apart during the terrible earthquake of 1953 when up to eight hundred people lost their lives. This scar on the landscape served as a reminder of past tragedy and the ever-present threat of future earthquakes, which have always haunted the island.

The climb was almost over as the gradient finally levelled out, allowing me to catch my breath and regain some composure. At this height, the climate was cooler, allowing the vineyards on my left to thrive. Further along this narrow road were a few houses belonging to local people. We were far away from the tourist areas. Eventually, I arrived at another main road. Over the years, I have always admired a beautifully maintained vegetable garden on this corner. The owner obviously cherished his large patch of land, and the tomatoes he grew would have won awards at any garden show back home. On my last run, I was so sad to see that this garden had literally gone to seed. The fruit and vegetables were gone, replaced with a mass of weeds. The gardener had probably passed away during the pandemic, which had been rife here as it was worldwide. 'How very sad', I thought to myself, as I continued on my way.

From here, I turned right, to follow the road towards the resort of Kalamaki. It was a long, straight road, and once again, I had to be on my guard for any kamikaze coach driver intent on death and destruction, or at the very least, with the sole aim of delivering forty-nine tourists to the airport on time! Initially, the road was relatively quiet, apart from the coaches. As I got closer to the resort, I ran past families making their way from the outlying hotels into the village and the beach. On one run, I noticed something lying at the side of the road. I almost ran past it, but something made me stop. At first, I thought it was a discarded toy. On closer inspection, I saw it was a small clutch bag. I opened it, and to my surprise, there were five passports and a very large amount of cash inside. It was someone's very unlucky day. I looked at each passport, trying to find a contact number. Unfortunately, there were none in any of the passports, nor was there any contact information in the bag. Clutching the bag, I continued my run. Fotis, my brother-in-law, would know what to do; I was very reluctant to hand over this amount of cash to anyone else. Fotis always knew what to do for the best.

Ten minutes later, I was running down the main street of Kalamaki. Tourists were everywhere. It was a busy time in the morning. I overtook a very distressed elderly lady pushing what was obviously her grandchild in a pushchair. She was crying and looking around her in great distress. Of course, this caught my attention, but what really surprised me was the fact that I recognised her. I could not think where I had seen her before for a moment, and then it suddenly twigged. I had her passport in the bag I was carrying. I stopped and walked over to her. She was busy crying and scanning the gutters at the same time.

"Excuse me," I said. She looked up at me and then continued searching and crying. I held up her bag and asked if this would help her stop crying. It's not often that I can make someone's day, but today was the day to make a difference in someone's life. She literally let out a scream and hugged me, really hugged me. To lighten the moment, I said that I had spent all her money, but I had trouble selling the passports so she could have those back. She hugged me even tighter and laughed.

She then went into detail about how she had lost the bag. She and her family had arrived that morning. The toddler would not sleep, so she had volunteered to walk into town and change all their holiday money into euros. That done, she put the bag into the bottom of the pushchair. On arrival back at the hotel, she was devastated when she realised that the toddler had thrown the bag out of the pushchair. She had been retracing her steps for the last hour. She was too scared to return without it. A great piece of advice formulated that day is to make sure you add your mobile phone number to the emergency contact details on the back of your passport. It could literally save your day and your holiday. There, that alone justifies the money you spent on this book.

Leaving my new best friend behind, I continued my run. At this point, I could see how the fortunes of this island had changed over the years since I had first started to visit. So many empty shops and restaurants were falling into disrepair and decay. People's broken dreams and lost futures were on display, and the sadness was palpable. One empty restaurant, in particular, caught my eye. It was called The Lighthouse, and I remember it opening only a few years earlier. The owners were English and had spent much time and money on the property. It now stood empty, and the weeds were already reclaiming everything. How desperately sad, a testament to broken dreams.

Finally, I came to the end of the street and followed the road past the Crystal Beach Hotel, set as it is directly on the beachfront. Thank goodness this still seems to be doing well, as evidenced by new additions to the original hotel, such a beautiful spot for a holiday. The road winds past a small cliff proudly displaying the Greek flag. Half of this cliff collapsed onto the beach just a few years ago. The rubble still blocks the shoreline and probably will forever. The Greeks tend to leave things as they are.

I ran onwards towards another traditional restaurant that happily has not changed in the last forty years. And then, just as quickly as I had entered the tourist zone, I was back out into the wilderness. There were just a few hotels dotted around. Thankfully, no high-rise buildings were permitted because of the famous and protected Loggerhead turtles who returned to the island's beaches every year to lay their eggs. These hotels tended to blend nicely into the background. Once I passed these hotels, I was well and truly back in time, to the Zante of old.

I ran past a small number of old, half-tumbled-down houses, still occupied by the generation of villagers who fought in the Second World War. They have seen tourism explode over the last forty to fifty years. I watched over the years as these residents tended their small gardens, sit in shade, and watch the world, or at least a solitary runner, go by. Little had changed in their world over the decades except that the owners of these properties were slightly more bent and slightly less mobile with the passing of each year.

Ahead of me, I saw a very old man come out of a shack, for that is all it was, and shuffle across the path to his small but perfectly tended vegetable patch. There was an old blue dining chair sitting at the side of the garden. As he reached it, he held onto one side and slowly lowered himself onto the chair. I was still fifty yards away when I heard him making strange clicking sounds. As if by magic, chickens suddenly appeared, running from all directions towards the old man. He thrust a hand into his old baggy trousers and produced pellets, which he scattered at his feet. Occasionally, he bent down to stroke one of his pets, for pets, they most definitely were. He dropped a few pellets onto his trousers, and one of the chickens fluttered up onto his lap. As a reward, she received more pellets and a gentle stroke of her head.

A warm fuzzy feeling enveloped me as I drew level with the ancient man. 'This is how it should be', I thought to myself. 'Man and nature at one and living in perfect harmony together'. I raised my hand in greeting to this kind, caring, gentle old man. I then saw one of his hands move quickly, very quickly, in what I initially thought was in response to my greeting.

Instead of waving, his hand held the chicken's head and, in one swift movement, twisted it almost off the chicken's shoulders. It all happened so quickly and quietly that the remaining chickens continued to eat at his feet. I was stunned, and so shocked that I had to stop and just look as the old chap slowly got to his feet and shuffled back to his hut carrying the recently killed chicken by its feet. Everything had happened at such lightning speed that it was difficult to believe that a chicken had just been dispatched for his Sunday lunch. At first, I felt saddened to have seen death arrive so swiftly and silently that none of his chickens had even noticed. Even the dead chicken had no idea that it had just been killed, and I guess that was the point.

Every year, millions of poor birds are kept in appalling conditions and massacred inhumanely without thought or feeling. This chicken had led a perfect life and had been dispatched by someone who obviously cared for and respected it. I have been a vegetarian for over four decades, but even I had to admit to myself that if you have to eat meat, there can be no more acceptable way to do it. I continued my run with mixed feelings. My overactive imagination now had this pensioner as a Greek resistance fighter, dispatching the enemy just as swiftly and quietly. Who knows, I may well have been right. Sadly, I will never know. As I ran past his house the next year, the garden was overgrown, and the blue chair had gone. There were no chickens. I just hoped that his release had been as swift and painless as the one he gave his pets.

Now, I was headed back towards the tourist shops and hotels. As I watched the sunburnt, sweaty and pretty obviously underactive tourists making for the all-day drinking bars, I wondered if they had any idea of the history and way of life that existed so close to where they were staying. As the majority were heading for the bars advertising full English breakfasts and cheap beer, I hazarded a guess that probably, they didn't.

My run now took me along the main road towards Laganas, the island's notorious hot spot. Luckily for me, I turned right onto a single-lane road long before I got there. This road took me back to the airport, just yards from the runway. If I timed it right, I could race a landing aircraft and wave to the crew and passengers. Try that at Gatwick! Finally, I ran past a couple of farms, the residents of which had taken to murdering each other with shotguns, quite a notorious vendetta and well known to the locals on the island. Luckily for me, they didn't seem to hold a grudge against tourists or runners. Finally, I panted my way back to the beautiful villa-style house where Sally, Fotis and my niece Emilia lived. Sliding back the large metal gate, I was greeted by a pack of five dogs. All but one were happy to see me. I bent down to pat their heads whilst Abbie, the only dog who didn't like me, slunk away into a corner. 'That is family', I thought to myself, 'you can't please everyone'. I always felt immense satisfaction when I had completed the run that I have been lucky enough to be doing for nearly forty years. Long may it continue

Chapter 27

That's Amore

I flew the Boeing 747 for the majority of my career. As it was a long-haul aircraft, it only ever flew to far-away places. Sitting on the flight deck one day, I stared out at the scene below as once again, we flew over Europe on our way to some far-flung destination. I realised that I only ever flew over Europe, never to it. All my European running adventures were confined to the holidays I enjoyed there. The most memorable run, for all the wrong reasons, was the run I did the day before my eldest son, James, got married. Never mind the bride not turning up; typically, it was me that nearly did not make the wedding.

We were staying in a castle near Milan, Italy. This was not just any old castle. It was the 'Castello' where my son was about to marry the beautiful Carlotta. The venue had not been chosen randomly. It just happened to be one of the properties owned by Carlotta's parents. As you might have already guessed, James was marrying into the Italian aristocracy. Liz and I could not have been more delighted that he was joining such a wonderful, kind, and caring family. The wedding was due to be held over three days. Guests from all over the world were arriving for what was to be an extraordinary event, very nearly spoiled by an idiot. By now, you can probably guess which idiot it was.

The castle is set amid rice fields to the west of Milan. This area is famous for its risotto rice. Equally famous is the irrigation system designed by none other than Leonardo Da Vinci. Well, he may have been quite good at painting, designing, inventing and just about everything else he put his mind to. But from first-hand experience, I can assure you that he was pretty inept at creating an irrigation system that runners can also enjoy.

We were all gathered together the day before the wedding, milling around the grounds. We were admiring the last-minute finishing touches to the preparations. The whole vista was quite exquisite and felt more like a royal wedding. I have never been to such an event before, and after my performance, I doubt I will ever be invited to one again.

Despite the number of workers busily doing this and that, we all had our own little jobs to do. Mine was the most straightforward. Carlotta had created beautiful wooden signs to be placed around the gardens to direct guests to the various events taking place, a task that she cleverly realised should not have placed too big a responsibility on my shoulders. More guests were arriving that day, and a formal lunch was being prepared in the main hall.

This was my eldest son's wedding, and an extraordinary amount of time and money was spent making the weekend perfect. I should have completed my assigned task, placed the signs in the appropriate places and gone for a shower before our guests arrived. To be fair to myself, I did consider doing this, but sadly, not for long enough. Instead, I had a flash of inspiration.

Why not go for a run instead? What harm could a little run do, especially as I had two hours to play with before the guests arrived?

I could run, plant the signs, shower, and still have plenty of time to prepare for lunch. I was so pleased with my plan, I sought out my family and announced my intentions. Stony faces greeted my news, and stern advice not to do anything so daft was freely shared. With my best reassuring smile, I tried to convince them of the brilliance of my idea. Despite their objections, well-founded as it turned out, I set off into the surrounding rice fields, very nearly never to be seen again.

I had checked and rechecked my route very carefully. I'd left nothing to chance as I had to be back within the hour. By my reckoning, the run should have taken no more than forty minutes. I was safe. Unbeknownst to me, there was trouble ahead, serious trouble. Large wild creatures, that had no right to be there, were awaiting my arrival. Hidden away, they lay in wait for any unexpecting wedding guest to venture into their territory.

As I set off, I was, of course, totally unaware of what lay ahead. It was going to be all plain sailing and an excellent opportunity to enjoy a lovely run in new surroundings. The castle was isolated, over five kilometres from any main road. There were a few settlements connected with no more than dusty tracks. To the first of these, I set off at what must be said was a cracking pace. I boasted to myself that I could probably do the whole run in thirty minutes as I quickly bore down on my first turning point. I was running alongside man-made irrigation channels designed and created all those centuries ago.

Little wooden gates were used to increase and decrease the water supply. It was almost impossible to believe these were artificial waterways; they blended so perfectly with their surroundings. Herons flew lazily above, trying to spot any unsuspecting fish. Various other aquatic birds flitted in and out of the rice plants as I continued on my way.

The first hamlet I came to consisted of a small church and about twenty houses. It took me less than three minutes before I was back out into the surrounding farmland. I checked Google maps on my phone and I was definitely on the correct route. I should have been passing what looked like a football pitch in another few kilometres. Sure enough, right on cue, there was the pitch; although obviously no football had been played there this century, a football pitch it most certainly was or had been. There would be a turning to the right in about ten minutes. After that, a small track would lead me directly back to the castle and a well-deserved lunch.

Checking my watch, I calculated that I would have time not only to erect the signs and have a shower, but I would have time for a cheeky beer as well. The sun shone, birds tweeted, and all was well with my world. As you can guess, this feeling of euphoria was not to last very long.

Sure enough, the turning to the right appeared just as I had calculated. I turned and ran down it with a spring in my step. The road quickly descended into a track, the track soon became a field, and the field quickly became a waterway. This, most certainly, was not in my plan.

I stopped; there was little else I could really do except swim. Looking at my phone, the little blue dot had me in the right place. I must have missed something, a turning I had probably overlooked. I turned around and ran back to the road. Looking around, I realised there were no other tracks or paths near where I was now standing. Feelings of dread quickly replaced my previously sunny disposition. Again, I ran back to where the trail disappeared into the waterway. The landscape in this part of the Lombard region was flat, with no hill anywhere in sight. On a clear day such as this one, the outline of the Alps could just be made out. I stood scanning the horizon and could see the castle's vast roof in the distance. So close, yet so far. Looking at my watch, I noticed that I had been running for nearly an hour.

Backtracking had taken longer than I had realised. A quick calculation convinced me that I did not have time to turn around and retrace my run. I had to keep going forward if I had any chance of making lunch. I could not bear to think of the consequences if I was late. Everyone except me had gone to extraordinary lengths to make it a perfect weekend.

There was no way I could be late or, even worse, miss lunch altogether. I had to go where no man had probably ever gone before. I had to cross the canals and irrigation ditches. There really was no other way I could get back in time for lunch.

The first canal was quite wide. What was dear old Leonardo thinking? I just hoped that it was not as deep as it was wide. Of course, Italian engineering geniuses do not do things by half. I found myself swimming across, holding my phone above my head as I went. Memories of Zanzibar flashed into my mind, as did memories of the rice fields in Narita. Both of those runs had ended poorly, and I did not hold out much hope for this run either.

After I pulled myself up the bank on the other side, I ran diagonally across the field to the next water obstacle. Into the water I went once again and out the other side. Each time, I collected more grass and debris on my clothes and shoes. I kept looking at the castle. It seemed to be getting farther away. If you are ever tempted to run through a rice field, please don't; it is not as much fun as it might seem. Also, it's very, very messy. Very quickly, you start to resemble the creature from the lagoon. The mud sticks to you like glue; the water seems to add to the accumulation, not remove it.

And then things suddenly and almost unbelievably got a whole lot worse. I entered yet another large tributary and set off with my now well-rehearsed one arm swimming style, the other holding my phone in the air. This put me in a very vulnerable position for what was about to happen next on this nightmare run.

Almost one hundred years before I started my run, some not-so-clever Italian decided to introduce a South American beaver, the Nutria or Coypu, into this delicate ecosystem. His idea had been to farm these creatures for their fur. Instead, they escaped and ran riot in the rice fields, growing to an alarming and unnatural size. They had no natural predators to keep their growth rate in check. Of course, I had no idea that they even existed, until two of them swam out of the reeds and headed directly for me.

If you are already highly stressed and anticipating a severe dressing down in the not-too-distant future, the last thing you can cope with is a pair of large rodents heading your way. As far as I was concerned, I was about to be attacked by a plague of giant rats. Well, that is precisely what they looked like to me. I was panic-stricken. I'm not too fond of rats; in fact, I really hate them. I can just about tolerate tame white rats, but the ones I really object to are the big brown disease-ridden wild ones, such as the ones bearing down on me. I turned and swam as fast as I could. More of these disgusting creatures appeared from the banks and joined their comrades in chasing me. I was in rat hell. They all seemed to be intent on catching and biting me. "Dear God help me", or something to that effect, I screamed as I pulled myself back onto semi-dry land.

I lay there on my back with my heart rate going through the roof. I kept a very keen watch on the bank to ensure I wasn't being followed. Luckily, the water seemed to be their domain, not the land. Eventually, I stood up and looked for another way back to the castle. There was nowhere else for me to go. I was surrounded by giant rat-infested water. How was I to know they were beavers? I certainly did not want to get close enough to ask them.

I stood there for what seemed an eternity, praying for a brainwave to help me decide what to do. Did I turn around and swim back the way I had come hoping there were no more rats? Or did I face my worst fears and carry on? Suddenly, I had a very clear vision of how angry Liz would be if I missed that first family meal. That galvanised me into action, and without another moment's hesitation, I plunged back into the rat's lair.

The next twenty minutes were some of the worst times I have ever experienced. In each stream, there lurked the prospect that I might be attacked. I tried to make as much noise as possible to frighten them away. It seemed to work as finally, I pulled myself out of the last ditch and ran the last kilometre back to the bosom of my loving family. I say loving; there was not much love in evidence as I stumbled into the dining hall.

The table had been set beautifully, and eleven family and friends were seated, finishing the remains of what looked like a wonderful feast. There was an empty seat at the head of the table reserved for the groom's father. As I walked into the hall, all conversation stopped, and eleven pairs of eyes bore into me. These were my new relatives, most of whom I had yet to be formally introduced to.

Suddenly, I realised that I was leaving an ever-increasing puddle of muddy water on the beautiful flagstone floor. My mouth opened, but for once in my life, no words were forthcoming. I was still in shock at being almost eaten alive by giant rats, I needed love and sympathy, and by the look on my wife's face, I was not about to receive either.

Finally, I managed to splutter an apology. I tried to explain my near-death experience. I could see the disbelief in everyone except for Andrea, Carlotta's remarkable father. Standing up, he told the story of the imported beavers and how intimidating they can appear if you do not know what they are. I could have kissed him.

I beat a hasty retreat to shower and re-join the group as quickly as possible. An hour later, I was sitting in the sunshine with the meal Elena, Carlotta's equally wonderful mother, had saved for me. Everyone seemed to have forgiven me, and laughter rang around the courtyard as I recounted my Indiana Jones-type adventure. Of course, each time I retold the story, the beavers became larger and the terror more terrifying. Liz took a lot more convincing but eventually, I was forgiven. Belatedly, I placed all the signs; around the grounds. Some were even in the correct place.

I was banned from running for the rest of the weekend, which, to be fair, was what I deserved. I saved my energy for the tennis tournament on the Sunday which Rob, my younger son, and I, somehow managed to win!

That night, I could not sleep; those giant rats were still out there waiting for revenge. Beavers indeed! My new best friend Andrea couldn't fool me. I know a giant rat when I'm chased by one.

Chapter 28

Two Weeks in Provence

Bonnieux is an idyllic French town set high above rolling fields of lavender, quintessentially French in every sense of the word. The town was a fortified village looking across the Vaucluse valley to the equally beautiful town of Lacoste.

We were lucky enough to have been invited by a good friend to stay at his villa. This magnificent property was set in its own grounds. To get there, you had to drive down a rough track, about a mile from the town. The property was very remote and set high up on a hillside. It had panoramic views over the valley, a perfect place to relax and enjoy the scenery. There was also a swimming pool and cherry tree orchard.

My friend knew all about the local area and warned me of the dangers posed by the wild boars, who roamed freely in the surrounding hills. Such were the dangers they posed; he suggested that I should always keep to the tracks and avoid wandering too far into the woodlands.

That first morning, I sat looking at local maps, trying to find a circular run I could enjoy from the house. It was a beautiful early summer morning. We sat in the shaded courtyard of the villa. The remains of breakfast sat on the enormous wooden table. We had just finished the freshly squeezed orange juice and the last of the home-made croissants. The family were making their way to the large swimming pool, the morning sun glinting off the water, making it almost impossible to resist a quick swim, except of course, for yours truly.

Instead of following the family to the pool, I was busy tying my shoelaces. I had found a running route and could not wait to see if it would live up to my high expectations. Suncream was being applied liberally as I ran past the family and onto the dirt track that marked the start of my run. Shouts of "be careful" and "see you later if the wild boar don't get you," rang in my ears as I set off down the track.

Being set so high on the escarpment, the only sensible route was to go down, and I found myself running down a steep path. There was a good-sized gite or small cottage in the villa's grounds. It had once been home to the workers who had tended to the house, orchard and gardens. Sadly, it had fallen into disrepair, and nature had started to reclaim it. Apparently, there were plans afoot to renovate this charming building. I hoped they would start soon as nature was quickly winning the battle.

As I left our accommodation behind, the terrain quickly became more and more barren. There were harsh, wild gorse bushes just waiting to ensnare some unexpecting runner in their thorny grasp. 'Not today', I thought to myself smugly. 'I am going to be careful on this run'. Poking my tongue childishly at the bushes, I almost ran straight off the cliff's edge. Had I done so, I would have plunged vertically straight down onto a small row of houses two hundred metres below.

I had no idea that this cliff face was there. One moment, I was happily sprinting down the track; the next, the track ceased abruptly. One step further and a leap into the void would have been the last step I ever took. I was on the very edge, my arms windmilling in a desperate attempt to arrest my forward momentum. If you have ever run down a steep slope, you'll know how difficult it is to stop or change direction suddenly. That's how close I was to going over the edge. Had I plunged over the precipice, it would have been put down as an apparent suicide, either that or a lemming complex.

Heart pumping, hands shaking, body trembling, I looked down at the vertical drop onto the dwellings below. What would the homeowner think as a body slammed into their roof? Maybe, it had happened before, and they would simply scoop up my remains and put them in a pit with everyone else who had ever toppled over the cliff.

The sooner I got away from the place that had almost caused my demise, the better, and I backtracked to find where I had gone wrong. Sure enough, alongside those thorny bushes was a narrow track, the one I should have followed. Of course, the bushes had their revenge on the tongue-poking idiot this time. The thorns cut deeply into my bare arms and legs as I struggled along the ever-narrowing pathway. By the time I emerged onto a wider track, the blood flowed freely, and I looked like I had indeed, fallen over that cliff. 'How many of my runs ended up with me bleeding copiously?' I mused, as this more comprehensive pathway twisted and turned itself through the forest until eventually, it emerged onto a proper road. I turned around and stared up at the place where I had nearly toppled over. It was a long way up and equally a long way down, and I gave an involuntary shiver as I turned and started the long climb back up the hill.

The road slowly wound itself upwards, always upwards, back towards Bonnieux. 'Another run, another hill', I thought to myself. At least I had managed to escape being attacked by wild boar so far. It took me nearly an hour to fight my way back up the hill. I puffed my way to the beginning of the town. If I thought the road was steep, then I hadn't seen anything yet.

Bonnieux was built on the apex of the hill. It had started at the bottom many centuries ago and slowly expanded up the hill to the top. I followed those ancient builders as I made my way up to the main square. From here, the view was simply stunning. You looked out across the valley to Lacoste, another fortified town set on a hill. These towns were serious rivals in medieval times. Fortunately, they had learnt to live peacefully, side by side. Setting off once more, I struggled ever upwards. The streets are a sheer delight; there is something to see and marvel at on every corner of this ancient town. I ran along the main road until I came to the track leading back to our villa. It was then a very welcome, gently sloping run back to the family, still sitting by the pool.

I sat down, relieved that I was finally back safely. I had completely forgotten that I was covered in dried blood. I must have looked a proper sight. I started to invent a story of how I fought off a herd of wild boar when I was suddenly stung by a huge wasp. Swearing, I jumped straight into the pool, fully clothed. I am curious to know if wasps are attracted by blood. They certainly seemed to like mine. However, after that first sting, we were plagued by wasps for the rest of our stay.

We were back in Provence ten years later, but not at the same villa. That had been sold some years before. We were staying in St Julienne, another fortified town on a hill, just thirty minutes' drive from Bonnieux. The town itself is once again very isolated, just one road in and one road out. We arrived late in the afternoon and watched a glorious sunset from our elevated position. Well, whilst Liz watched the sunset, I was secretly planning my morning run. 'Best not to say anything and spoil the moment', I thought to myself. The weather that summer was breaking records all across Europe. Even the UK broke through the forty-degree barrier for the first time. I was tying my laces the following morning in beautiful sunshine, whilst being scowled at by my wife. I thought it was a bit hot to run, but there again, I had run in hotter weather than this, so I put that thought to the back of my mind.

I had planned a route along the main road for the first five kilometres. Then, I had found a trail through the thick woods back to the outer boundary of the town. Being naturally cautious and sensible, I had even drawn another little map, just in case my phone could not pick up a signal. This was a great idea. I was proud of myself for having gone to such lengths to ensure I did not get lost. It might have worked even better if I had not left my map on the breakfast table. That, however, was not the greatest of my problems that day.

Initially, the run went exactly to plan. I ran along the main road and followed its twisting and turning path down from the town. It must have been rush hour as I saw three cars rather than the typical solitary car. Roads in this part of France were ridiculously empty. The road straightened out, and as I came to the expected sharp right-hand bend, I saw the start of the track that would take me back to St Julienne. I set off down the path. Ten minutes later, I was hopelessly lost, again!

The pathway had divided in two and then, further along, into another two tracks. If I had thought the roads were quiet, this was like being on another planet. There was no sign of any human habitation or presence except for a few empty shotgun cartridges scattered liberally here and there. I just hoped that whoever fired these were local hunters of game and nothing more nefarious had taken place in this wilderness. Finally admitting defeat, I stopped to look at Google maps. I had wanted to do this the old-fashioned way but look at the trouble that had got me into. I held my phone in front of me and tried to work out exactly where I was. Naturally, there was no signal. What else did I expect out here?

Smiling to myself, I dug deep into both pockets in a vain attempt to produce the map I had drawn so carefully. Eventually, I resorted to pulling out my pockets, desperately attempting to locate my map. There was, of course, no map, that was sitting on the breakfast table.

Cursing loudly; there was no one to hear, so I could curse loudly, I looked around to try to work out which way I should go. I consoled myself with the thought that at least no giant rats were swimming after me, and I did not have a wedding lunch to get back for. This became a scant consolation as I was about to meet something that could actually kill me.

I chose the most likely-looking track and set off once again. I had been running for over an hour, and the sun was now at its zenith. In other words, it was hot! I was running uphill, which was a positive sign as the town was on top of a hill. I was running in thick woodland, but at least the track made my progress slightly easier. And then, I came to a huge villa. I turned a corner, and this lovely building was in front of me. How or why someone built it there, I had no idea. You could not possibly drive a vehicle to where I was now standing, and there were no signs that anyone had ever attempted to. Yet there was a newly built villa, totally deserted and isolated. At least I would have somewhere to sleep if I failed to get out of these woods.

I set off again, trying to think of a plausible excuse if or when eventually, I got back. I thought my map had probably been discovered by now and I would not be expected back anytime soon.

Suddenly, I heard what sounded like an express train crashing through the undergrowth. I had never heard anything even remotely similar. I looked around trying to trace the source of this commotion. Suddenly, a few feet in front of me, the ugliest creature I have ever seen smashed through the bushes and onto the path. Another few yards, and he would have run straight into me. He stopped and glared at me. I glared back but to be honest, I was terrified.

So this was the wild boar I had been warned about all those years ago. And then, another boar appeared, and then another. I had disturbed a family, and they were not in the least impressed. I stood utterly still. These creatures, with their fearsome and deadly horns, were swift. I had no chance of outrunning them. The large male then charged, thank God, back into the undergrowth and not towards me. The others quickly followed, and then they were gone, just like that. Silence returned.

Checking that I had not done anything inappropriate in my shorts, I got out of there as quickly as possible. Twenty minutes later, I found myself in a private orchard. I guessed it was private as I was being shouted at by an angry-looking old man. I was delighted, not at being yelled at, but by the vision in front of me. I could see St Julienne, still a long way in the distance, but I was definitely going the right way. I smiled at the grumpy old devil and set off as quickly as possible. Nearly an hour later, I finally panted my way back into our villa. I started to explain about the huge scary creatures in the forest. I explained that they were more dangerous even than the giant rats that had chased me in Italy. Recognising the danger signs, my wife's face said all I needed to know. This was a far more dangerous situation than facing wild boars or giant rats. I gave up on my excuses mid-sentence and sheepishly went to have a shower.

Chapter 29

Hitting the Home Run

Running was not something I did purely on my trips abroad. I ran every day at home or should that be every one of the few days I had at home. Earlier in my career, particularly, I would only be around for seven days every month. Liz brought up the boys almost single-handedly as, sadly, I was, for the most part, an absent father. I am incredibly proud of her achievement in producing two of the finest sons any parent could ever wish for.

So not only did Liz have to put up with me disappearing four times a month, but the very few days I was at home, I was typically found tying my laces and setting off on yet another run.

We are fortunate to live on the edge of the Ashdown Forest in West Sussex. This gives me a massive choice of running routes, great variety, and incredible views. So what do I do? I choose one specific area in the Gravetye Woods and run that daily. This run has everything I and any runner could want including woodland, lakes, hills, vineyards, and, to top it all, a vintage steam locomotive railway. I have three primary routes, which I interchange as much as possible. They vary in length from ten, the longest, then to eight and then five kilometres. Do not be misled by the seemingly short distance. These routes are over rough terrain and include some of the most challenging climbs I have ever endured. Well, maybe San Francisco is steeper, but only just!

I start at the same point for each, in a car park, and from there, I run through thick woodland. The pathway varies with the seasons, from concrete-like hardness in the summer to rivers of water in the autumn. These routes then turn into almost impassable mud baths in the winter. In the spring, the pathways can be all of these things simultaneously.

From my starting point, I head towards a long and punishing hill I have christened, 'Heartbreak Hill'. The name is pretty much an apt description of the torturous climb up onto the track leading to Gravetye Manor. This could be even more difficult after an autumnal storm when you have to climb over fallen trees. In the depth of winter, at the very apex of the final steep turn, black ice can quickly form. Despite knowing it was there, you still have to cross a river of ice before reaching the summit. This usually involves a fall or two and a lot of cursing. Once over the top of Heartbreak Hill, a single, track road winds gently down to the gates of Gravetye Manor. This beautiful old country manor had been tastefully converted into a luxury hotel with a Michelin-star restaurant. If you ever get the chance to go, take it. I promise you that you will not be disappointed. You may even see an old runner puffing towards the main gates. If you do, please beep and wave.

Just as I approach the ornate metal gates, I took a left turn and picked up a narrow track toward one of two lakes. The views back up towards Gravetye Manor are simply glorious. Whatever time of the year, there is always something new to see. Over the decades, I have become friends with the head gardener, Tom, who always gives me a friendly smile and a wave as I pass him. He also gives me some of the best tomato plants I have ever grown. The track leads steeply down to the lower lake, a totally unspoilt stretch of water that is difficult to describe unless you experience it yourself. This lake seems to live a life of its own. In the spring, swans, ducks and herons use the lake as a vast nesting ground. The tranquillity is almost perfect, and the small island in the middle makes the ideal nursery, away from the prying eyes and hunting skills of the large local fox and badger populations. The little wooden jetty that protrudes out from the bank provides the perfect launching pad for dogs and sometimes their owners as they seek refuge and a quick dip from the summer heat. In the autumn, wild raspberries hang temptingly on either side of the path. On cold winter mornings, occasionally, I have to stop running over the frozen ground to hurl a large log into the lake. This really does act as an icebreaker. I get rewarded as the grateful ducks launch themselves into the hole in the ice to find their breakfast. When running around this lake, life feels like it could not get any better. I am totally immersed in the moment.

From the lake, I head back into the woodland. The path now leads back up a muddy bank. It is here that I have my choice of routes. The lower path leads down to a creek and then up a long straight track back towards my car. If I take this option, my run lasts just over five kilometres. If I chose the ten-kilometre option. I turn right and continued up the ever-steeply rising hill. Halfway up, I make a sharp turn to the right and run directly up the steepest part of the embankment. Although only a short section, this part of the run feels like you need ropes and crampons rather than running shoes to get to the top. This is seriously steep. Parts of the route even rival San Francisco's roads!

My main concern is ensuring I do not run myself to an exhausted standstill. Halfway up, my legs are burning, and I am breathing hard. I have yet to meet anyone else daft enough to even walk up this track. If I do encounter anyone, I am not able to speak to them. I have no breath to spare for idle chatter. Hoof marks in the mud are a tell-tale sign that the only other users of this track are the numerous deer that call these woodlands their home. More often than not, I catch a glimpse of a herd of these splendid creatures. These are really wild deer, not the sort you see in Windsor Great Park. These animals shy away from any human contact. Sadly, the only time you can get close to them is when they have been hit by the ever-increasing number of cars on the local roads.

Finally, I reach the top of the embankment, now really struggling for breath. I make my way along a wide track. Here occasionally, I meet someone walking their dog. I usually scare the wits out of them as I resemble a madman suddenly appearing from the trees gasping for breath. I kid you not; I have actually made people scream in fright at the sight of me emerging onto the path. Of course, being breathless, I am entirely unable to reassure them that I was harmless. Instead, I try to give them a reassuring smile and quickly run off in the opposite direction.

Now, I follow this wide track until I reach another even wider one. This takes me on another steep climb, just what I need after what I have already pushed myself through. Finally, I reach the summit of my run. It is all downhill from now, apart from the three hills still to come. For now, the track levels out, and ten minutes later, I turn into another woodland area. From here, I turn down a bumpy path which resembles a dried-out riverbed. Running down here, I jump from one side of the bank to the other. It is exhilarating to accelerate down this section of the run, and it brings back memories of when I could run and swerve at this speed on a rugby field. Now, I need a fair downhill element to reach such speeds.

At the end of this track, I emerge into a large field which I cut across diagonally. The slope is still in my favour, and I maintain the illusion of speed. In early autumn, huge rolls of hay are be scattered around this field awaiting collection. I have a technique of running directly at a roll of hay, then launching myself at it. Turning in mid-air, I land on my shoulder and roll over the hay bale, and if all goes well, I land on my feet and continue my run without stopping. If it goes wrong, I end up on my backside looking silly. I have never met anyone else in this field, so the outcome does not really matter. Without worrying about anyone else's thoughts, I can make a complete fool of myself. Most importantly, it is just great fun.

Leaving my dignity behind, I pull the straw from my hair and continued along a driveway for a few hundred yards before turning again onto an uneven track. Climbing over a sizeable wooden sty, ahead there is another steep but short climb up and onto a railway track.

This is the Bluebell Railway, a well-known vintage steam engine heritage line that runs through Gravetye Woods. I stand there looking left and right before deciding that the coast is clear and it is safe to cross the single track. Many times, I hear the distant whistle of an approaching train. This is one of the few times I stop running and start watching. I cannot think of many places where you can get up this close and personal with a steam engine travelling at full speed. No health and safety here. It's just you and the train. The scene was reminiscent of the film, *The Railway Children* as I wave to the passengers.

On one memorable occasion, I puffed my own way up the embankment only to be met by about twenty people waiting at the top. I had never previously seen anyone at this spot, so I was confused as to why this crowd had formed. A few started to clap me as I reached the crossing. Smiling, I waved back. Suddenly, there was a loud whistle, much louder than the normal train whistle I was used to.

Immediately, I was ignored, and the crowd turned as one to look down the line; most had powerful cameras at the ready. From around the corner, spewing smoke, the Flying Scotsman roared into view. 'Wow, just wow', I thought to myself. I had no idea that the most famous train in the world, one hundred years old, was due to make an appearance. Had I been a minute later, I would have missed this historical sight. Sometimes, luck was on my side.

Once over the track, I run down the embankment into more woodland. Five minutes later, I am in the floodplain of the river Medway. In the winter, this is more like running in the river itself. Crossing the river on an ancient rickety bridge, I love the feeling as the bridge sways as I run across. Maybe, one day, I will regret subjecting the bridge to this treatment, but for now, it has never let me down.

Once across the bridge, there is another long steep climb up a rough, undulating field. Again, this is hard work. Getting to the top requires a lot of determination and effort. The large field is home to a few horses. They all stop and stare at the intruder in their home. One horse trots towards me and then joins me as I grunt and splutter my way to the top. Every time I run up this field, the same horse follows me, and we have become good friends. He only wants a good rub of his ears before I leave his domain. One day, I got to meet his owner and I was formally introduced to Vagabond, now my favourite horse.

Descending into the valley I am now in Kingscote Vineyard. On one side is the newly constructed barn; on the other, the Manor House. The vineyards climb the gentle hills on all sides, and a steam locomotive chugs its way through the valley.

I stop for a quick chat with the owner, Christen Mong before continuing my run. This has become a habit over the last few years. One day, after our usual chat I left Christen looking like a happy and contented man as I continued on my run. He never returned from that chat and cigarette break. He was struck down by a stroke and died on the way to the hospital. I still miss him and our chats.

Running through the vineyards was a real treat. As the seasons changed, I watched the vines put on their leaves, shimmer in the summer sunshine and produce their grapes. Harvest time was always enjoyable as teams of workers swarmed over the fields. Gone were the early days when friends of Christen rallied around to bring the harvest in.

Leaving the vineyard, I join a badly potholed road and ran the last few kilometres back to my car. The whole run is just over ten kilometres. I can think of nowhere else on earth where I could enjoy such beauty and contrast in such a short distance. On every run I set off in this beautiful part of the world, I never forget how lucky I am to live here.

236

Chapter 30

North of the Thames

There is another route that I have come to think of as a home run, the Wirral. Before meeting my wife, I had barely been north of the Thames. Birmingham seemed like another world, and Liverpool, well, I knew they had a pretty good football team and produced some excellent bands and singers. Apart from that, my knowledge was scant. Therefore, with a certain amount of trepidation, over thirty-five years ago, I set off to meet Liz's parents in a place called the Wirral, wherever that was!

Being a soft southerner, I was more than a little worried about the reception I would receive. I could imagine her father, with a flat cap, Woodbine, and stern look, dismissing me at first sight. I would probably not even be allowed over the threshold of their small, terraced house, set against the grimy backdrop of the decaying Liverpool Docks. I dreaded opening my mouth in public, fearing being set upon the moment the locals realised that I came from 'down south.'

Why, oh why, hadn't I just settled for someone from Sussex or Surrey? There would be no language or cultural barriers. I had heard people talking scouse and rarely understood half of what they were saying. My mood darkened the further north we drove. I didn't even know there was an M6 motorway until now.

Suddenly, we were on another motorway, the M56. I was now completely unsure of where we were. And then, to confirm my worst fears, there was a massive industrial monolith spewing out vast quantities of smoke on my right-hand side. This confirmed that I had been right about life north of the Thames. I had gone back in time to the Industrial Revolution. I sank deeper into my seat, gritted my teeth, and expected the worst.

Thirty minutes later, we pulled up outside a beautiful house on the seafront with unobstructed views across the Irish Sea. The promenade was wide and inviting. People were walking along, admiring the views. There was not a flat cap in sight. I was still apprehensive when the door opened, and I was welcomed like a long-lost son by my future in-laws.

Over the decades, I have grown to love the Wirral and the surrounding area. Liverpool is a wonderful city, and I can now understand some of what people say. It really is my second home, and I love the place. It is also a great place to go running.

The first time I mentioned that I may go for a little run along the promenade, my idea was met with approval from my future in-laws. What a splendid thing to do, they both agreed and even offered advice as to where to go. I liked these people. I liked them a lot.

And so off I ran, heading out along the promenade toward Leasowe Castle. Initially, the route took me along the promenade. On one side were houses, all large and highly individual residences. On the other side, the sea lapped onto the sandy shore. Soon, I left behind the houses and entered a sea wall with a comprehensive pathway on top to run along. There were now wide-open fields on the right which many years ago had been wild sand dunes. It wasn't easy to grasp just how diverse and dramatic the landscape was. This vast sea wall stretched as far as the eye could see. Eventually, the wall led off to the right, and I caught sight of Leasowe Lighthouse. The lighthouse no longer guided mariners safely towards the docks of Liverpool. However, it was beautifully maintained and still attracted tourists. As I passed the lighthouse, more green fields appeared, and the number of dog walkers increased as I approached Leasowe in the distance. People actually smiled and said hello. This really took me by surprise. Nobody ever really greeted you when I went running in Sussex. Suddenly, a golf course appeared and ran parallel to the sea wall. This was a real treat, as I enjoyed a game and watching others play.

Years later, I got to play a round of golf close by with my great friend Paul Casey. Golf is an expensive sport. In Sussex, a round can cost from forty pounds upwards. Most courses I have played have what is called 'Twilight' rounds. If you play late in the afternoon or early evening, there is a chance that it will get dark before you finish. Therefore, they only charge half the usual green fees. Being a cheapskate, that is my preferred option.

And so, with Paul standing behind me, looking slightly embarrassed, I politely asked if we could have two twilight rounds. The poor chap behind the counter looked blankly at me and shrugged his shoulders. He had no idea what I was talking about. I explained how such a round worked and asked if we could have a half-price round, as it was now late afternoon. He set off to ask the club secretary if this would be possible.

I turned to Paul and winked at him; these cheeky devils would not get away with charging us full price. Paul just stood looking at me. He appeared slightly embarrassed during the whole episode. I was made of sterner stuff. I was not troubled by any awkward feelings. This was simply a matter of principle. The cashier returned and advised me that they would make an exception and charge us twilight fees. I felt very proud of myself and produced my money, asking how much I owed. I had my twenty-pound notes at the ready.

"Err, that will be £5, please." I had just picked up two scorecards; these were free down south, but obviously not here. I was being charged £5 for them. Well, that was too much for a couple of pieces of cardboard, so I put them back. Despite this, he still asked for £5. I pointed out that I had returned the scorecards and just wanted to pay the green fees." Yeah, that'll be £5, please."

The penny, well pound, finally dropped. The green fee was £5 each, and I had been arguing over £2:50. I was so embarrassed that I paid the standard cost and left as quickly as possible. I don't think I left a particularly good impression of southern golfers behind me.

Continuing on with my run, I followed the golf course to Leasowe Castle now renovated into a rather nice hotel. I continued following the golf course until I reach the town of New Brighton. And then, it was time to turn around and retrace my steps, something I was not usually fond of doing. Here, however, it was different. The hills of North Wales now created a dramatic backdrop to the landscape. It was like starting a new and different run, especially as I could leave the pathway and run through the wetlands and sandhills, such a special place. I shared this new path with horse riders, some of whom I even managed to overtake. Finally, it was back to Liz and her family, just under fifteen kilometres of pure joy.

Now, I have grown to love the North, maybe even more than my wife does. The only downside is the weather. When they have inclement weather up north, they do it properly! On one infamous run, I reached my turning point in record time. I flew along at a pace I rarely ever achieved. The landscape flew past, and the deep dark clouds on the horizon mainly went unnoticed. I was having far too much fun. And then I turned around to run back the way I had just come.

The wind from the sea hit me full in the face with its northern ferocity. That was bad enough. Those clouds I'd previously ignored were obviously upset by my offhand and carefree attitude. They had come to remind me never to forget the potential the weather had to change in an instant. The hail arrived minutes after I had started my return run. I was now running into the teeth of a storm and a huge and really nasty storm. The hail stung my face, and the wind was so strong that it slowed my progress to a snail's pace. At one point, the wind was so ferocious that I had to jog, keeping one foot on the ground at all times. This kept me from being literally blown off my feet.

Eventually, I made it back, soaked, with my cheeks stung by a thousand hail stones, and exhausted. I had left on a bright sunny morning. It was not yet lunchtime, but the heavy rain and towering clouds had turned day to night.

Jim, my father-in-law, laughed at me. "If you think it's bad being on the shore when a storm hits, you should try being at sea."

Jim had served in the Merchant Navy, escorting the Atlantic Convoys, facing U-boats and the Arctic weather. I guessed he had a point, although it took me hours to get any feeling back into my extremities. This never happened at Gravetye, was my overriding opinion of that fearsome run.

I still look forward to that run, although sadly, both my in-laws have passed, and that beautiful house, my second home, has been sold to the next lucky inhabitants. They too, are very fortunate to live in such a wonderful part of the world.

Chapter 31

We All Fall Down

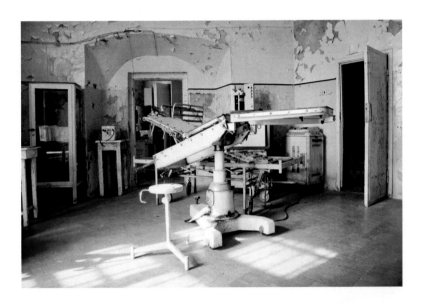

If you run on dirt tracks, at some point, you will fall. It's as simple as that. As sure as night turns into day, a runner will run into difficulty, sooner or later.

There are many ways you can fall. Slipping on wet ground, tripping over a tree root hidden by autumn leaves, stepping on a loose rock, all will have the same inevitable consequences: you will end up in an undignified heap on the ground. It took me only a short time to realise that the trick is not to try to avoid falling. That's impossible. It's how you fall that is the real life-saving trick.

The most dangerous part of a run is the downhill section. Here, you are usually at your fastest and most vulnerable. Take great care; once that dreaded out-of-control feeling hits you, the ensuing pain is never far away.

Luckily, I have been able to restrict the majority of my tumbles to flat or uphill terrain. In these situations, at least you have some degree of control over how you will go down. Still, if you are able to employ the correct technique, you can avoid some of the more serious consequences of unexpectedly arriving flat on the ground.

The worst thing you can do is put your hands out straight in front of you to save yourself. If you do this, you will end up with a broken wrist and shredded hands, and that's an optimistic outcome. The way to do it, and I have a lot of experience in this, is to rotate your body as you start to feel yourself falling. This has two advantages, Firstly, your hands and wrists are protected, and secondly, you land on the part of your anatomy that can better withstand the impact, your upper arms and shoulders. Witness soldiers parachuting into fields. They land feet first and then roll onto their shoulders. If you practise this enough, and by golly, I have, you can translate your fall into the most graceful of movements. I have been running, tripped, fallen forward, rolled onto my shoulder and used the momentum to regain my footing and carry on without stopping. I admit that it needs a lot of luck, but I have performed this in front of crowds on more than one occasion. I tried it in Central Park as I attempted to overtake a group of runners. I drew up alongside them, took my eyes off the road for a second and hit the curb. Down I went, rolled onto my shoulder and straight back up onto my feet. I continued my overtaking, hardly missing a stride. God knows what they thought they were witnessing. Who gets overtaken by an idiot who does a simultaneous victory roll?

But it really does work. Give it a try sometime, preferably in your back garden with no one looking rather than in Central Park. You are more likely to retain your dignity that way. Occasionally, it is impossible to avoid injury. Philosophically, it is just part of offroad running that you have to accept.

I am still running the equivalent of a marathon a week at sixty-five years of age. I have been running almost every day for over forty years, and everything works just as it used to. Maybe a little slower, but it still works.

The more serious injuries I have sustained, funnily enough, have not come from falling down. Rather, they have occurred whilst in the motion of running. Sure, I have tripped and gashed my hands, elbows and knees. Parts of my extremities look more like a pizza topping than a body part, but these have never stopped me from running. Only recently, I fell and badly gashed my knee. I got up and ran through the pain, which quickly dissipated thanks to the surge of endorphins, the best friends of runners everywhere. As I ran out of the woods towards my car, I could not understand why people in the car park were staring at me. Everything became apparent when I looked at myself when I got home. I had one brown leg and one red one, and blood was everywhere. It looked horrendous. Think *Texas Chainsaw Massacre*, and you will get the idea. I went over to the outside hose and washed my leg down. As the red river disappeared into the gutter, I put a strip of plaster onto the wound and carried on with my day. The real problems come unexpectedly, and their consequences can be far-reaching and prolonged.

Many years ago, I was out running in Antigua. The weather was hot, and the road was in its normal treacherous condition. There were potholes everywhere, and I had just avoided a particularly nasty one when my left ankle went straight into its smaller brother. Immediately, I knew I was in trouble. The searing pain left me with no doubt that I had sustained a serious injury. I did not fall. I just hopped around, cursing loudly. I was on a deserted road, so I had no choice but to turn back and make my way back to the hotel.

Once there, I called the reception desk and asked for a doctor to be sent to my room. The hotel only accommodated our crews, and the company paid for any medical needs. An hour later, the doctor was sitting on my bed, trying to rotate my ankle. My swearing and threats of violence persuaded him to discontinue this treatment. Suitably chastised, he called for a taxi to take me to the nearest hospital. With that, he quickly departed. I guessed I must have scared him a little.

Two hours later, clutching my X-rays, I hobbled down a corridor and sat outside the doctor's surgery, waiting to be called in to learn my fate. Suddenly, the door opened, and a nurse beckoned me inside. All these years later, I still find it difficult to believe the scene that greeted me.

The doctor was performing a foot amputation right in front of me. He looked over his shoulder and assured me he would not keep me waiting much longer. I have no idea how much longer he would have kept me. I have never hopped so far and so fast! I hailed a taxi and went straight back to my hotel, shaken and definitely stirred.

One of the crew went to the local chemist, and between us, we bound up my ankle as best we could manage. Then, I rang the British Airways operations desk in London and asked for a replacement pilot to be sent out. Fortunately, we were not due to fly home for another three days, so there was plenty of time for a replacement to be found.

Unfortunately, this new pilot arrived but was struck down by a bout of food poisoning. The flight was delayed for eight hours whilst a second replacement was found. As I sat there, fortunately, in First Class, the new pilot apologised for the delay to the flight. He then informed everyone that the delay was due to the original pilot breaking his foot. I received death stares from everyone around me. 'How unfair, but to plead my innocence would only make matters worse', I thought to myself. Instead, I settled back and continued to chat with my fellow passenger. One of the crew told me that her name was Helena Christensen, the supermodel. I thought she was rather attractive. As I pushed my seat back into its fully reclined position, I closed my eyes and smiled. 'This was the only chance

I would ever have to sleep with a supermodel', I laughingly thought to myself.

I went to my local hospital when finally, I got home. This time the doctor was not performing serious surgery in his office, and he informed me that I had a fractured ankle. He put my ankle in plaster and advised me not to run for a while after the plaster came off. I obeyed his advice to the letter. Just not the correct letter. I gave it a few days, bought myself an ankle brace and set off for a run. I kept that ankle brace on for nearly a year before I could run without it. Probably, I was stupid to run so soon after the injury, but in the long run, it turned out okay, and I didn't have to lose many weeks of running. Thank goodness my doctor never found out.

Muscle injuries can be far more painful and more persistent. I tore a calf muscle simply by running too far. The pain was excruciating, preventing me from running for over a month. To this day, I dread the thought of that pain ever recurring. My most recent injury, which has been plaguing me for nearly two years, is my torn hamstring.

Again, the injury at first was very low-key. I was coming to the end of my run when I felt a slight twinge at the top of the back of my leg. I rubbed the affected area whilst continuing with my run. Once I got home, I continued to massage the rear part of my thigh. It was painful but not significantly so. The real pain was waiting in abeyance until I started to run the following day.

Two minutes after I set off, it felt like someone, using a blunt knife, was trying to strip the muscle from the back of my leg. The pain was severe enough for me to cry out in agony. It really was that bad. Two years later, despite treatment, it still plagues me. I was only immobile for two months, but my leg still hurts. Oddly enough, the pain is worse when I am stationary, especially sitting as a passenger in a car. It is most comfortable when I am running. You can guess what I prefer to do.

The nagging injuries come and go, but like the song *Three Wheels on My Wagon*, I keep rolling along. At my age, if I stopped for every ache and pain, I would never run again.

Some days, I look out of the window and see a cold, grey, wet day. I am tempted to stay indoors. Why push myself on such a day? While I ponder this question, I often start to put on my running gear. By the time I am ready, I have forgotten what I was thinking about. Noticing that I have my running gear on, I set off without further thought. Old age sometimes has its advantages.

Running is also a perfect barometer for deciding how unwell I am. If I start with a cough and a sneezing fit, and I can still run, it's merely a cold. If I actually have the flu, the idea of a run becomes unthinkable, and I will skulk away into a dark room and wait until I feel better. The best thing about this is that if I do not go for my daily run, the family immediately knows that I am really unwell. I get sympathy rather than ridicule for the so-called man flu.

Keeping very active over the years has helped me cope with life. I am by no means complacent. I could be one injury away from ending my running career. Hopefully, that will not happen anytime soon. In the meantime, I will continue and absolutely enjoy doing what I know works for me.

Chapter 32

All I Want is a Room Somewhere

I was twenty-seven miles from home. It was a cold and dark night. Unsurprisingly, I was about to make a very poor decision.

Along with a group of friends, we had hired a minibus to take us to see a concert by *M People* at the Brighton Arena. Heather Small had been belting out her string of hits, and we were all having a great time. The minibus was waiting for us as we left the concert. It had been a fun night, but I was more than ready to go home. I had only landed that morning and was looking forward to a good night's sleep.

Suddenly, one of the group came up with a new plan, why not go to a nightclub? The night was still young and so where the majority of the group. There was only one dissenting voice, and nobody was interested in what I had to say. The bus driver was seduced with an offer of more money, and the continuation of the night was signed and sealed. On the other hand, I wanted to avoid going to a nightclub. After a bit of disagreement with my wife, I declared that I would get the train home. I had an unrealistic hope that this would persuade the others to abandon their new plans, but no such luck. I stood there as they all piled into the bus and disappeared into the frosty night.

'Well, that hadn't gone as well as I had hoped,' I thought to myself, as I turned and headed towards the station. It was only a mile away. Still, half-expecting our bus to turn back at any minute and pick me up, eventually, I arrived at the station, a very closed railway station. It was deserted, with no bus, train, taxi, or minibus in sight. Well, this made my situation a little more complicated. In those days, I did not own a mobile phone. They were only just starting to become popular. However, there was no coverage where we lived, so I could see no reason to buy one. They probably would never erect phone masts in rural areas and confidently, I predicted that the whole idea of mobile phones would never catch on and eventually, be forgotten.

Still, that was not my current problem. My problem was that I was twenty-seven miles from where I lived. I had very little money on me and no obvious way of getting home. I was also bloody freezing. Suddenly, a solution to my problems hit me through my slightly intoxicated brain. Of course, I could run home. I had run a marathon before, and this was only a mile longer than a marathon, and what's a mile between friends?

Had I been able to debate this idea with anyone with a modicum of sense, they would have pointed out that I was not suitably dressed for such an endeavour, neither did I have any running shoes. Along with that it was pitch black, and the temperature was about minus seven degrees centigrade. Sadly, these details eluded me as I broke into a trot and headed off into the night.

Initially, all went well. The alcohol pumping around my body was still protecting me from the full impact and implications of what I had decided to do. Throwing my toys out of the pram when deciding not to go to the nightclub was still uppermost in my mind, and I was still aggrieved that I had been left alone to stew in my own grumpiness.

After about thirty minutes of hard running, I was beginning to sober up. My feet were starting to protest at my choice of footwear. I considered turning around and trying to find the nightclub where everyone was warm and enjoying more drinks. Sadly, I was too proud to admit that I had acted like a spoiled child, so I continued.

An hour later and I was not making significant progress. I was running along the main Brighton to London road. Luckily, there was a good cycle track that I could follow that ran alongside the road. By now, the full impact of my ridiculous decision was really hitting home. Apart from aching feet, I was now extremely cold. I was shivering and rubbing my arms to generate some warmth.

The usual Christmas films had started being pulled out of the archives and rerun for the umpteenth time. We had watched Audrey Hepburn as Eliza Doolittle in *My Fair Lady* only the day before. One memorable scene had her walking down a cold street, singing, ''All I want is a room somewhere, far away from the cold night air, oh wouldn't it be loverly.''

Songs have a habit of sticking in your head, and you cannot get rid of them. It's really annoying. A modern term for this phenomenon is an 'earworm.' This time, the song fitted perfectly with my current predicament, and it became my earworm. I sang it repeatedly. It really helped to keep my spirits up.

Another hour later, I was still plodding along the main road. My feet had stopped hurting. They were now too cold to feel any pain. Surprisingly, I had managed to warm up a little. I was keeping up a respectable pace for someone so inappropriately dressed, and that generated its own heat.

Another hour later, I was still not even halfway home. It was now three in the morning, and the temperature had dropped even further. It was too cold to even snow, which was to my advantage. My earworm was doing its best to keep my mind off what I was attempting to do. There was now no traffic at all. Even the main roads were completely devoid of any vehicles. I took the opportunity to run in the middle of the road. It made things a little easier. The clouds had parted, and I was now running in a spooky deserted moonlit landscape. At least, I could see where I was going now, and I managed to increase my pace.

Two hours later, five hours after leaving Brighton, I ran along narrow country lanes, leaving the main roads behind me. I could have been in a better place, both physically and geographically. I was in a very different place from where I had expected to be when I set out to enjoy a concert the previous evening. I knew that I was approaching the limit of my endurance. I also knew that I could not stop. If I did that and sat down in the middle of nowhere, there was a serious chance that hypothermia would ensure that I would never get up again. I had to keep going. Only ten miles to go. Maybe I could make it after all.

Another hour later, and even my earworm had finally left me; it had probably found that warm room. I was really now totally alone. There were still five miles between me and the warmth of home. I was now approaching Worth School, a large private school where the submarine periscope was invented. I had no idea why that useless thought had popped into my mind. The next thought was much more helpful. I remembered that there was a red public telephone box just outside the school entrance. Even better news was that I had some change in my pocket. 'Who needs mobile phones?' I thought to myself, as the telephone box came into view.

It was now approaching six o'clock in the morning. It was dark, although the moon provided enough light to see the white and frosty landscape. With trembling fingers, I began to dial home. I waited and waited, but there was no answer. I could not hang up as I had no plan B. If I could not get through, I would have to keep ringing until someone answered. After what seemed an eternity, I heard Liz's sleepy yet concerned voice. My hands were trembling so much that I could not get my coins into the slot to complete the call. I kept dropping the coins and bent down to retrieve them. Please, please don't hang up, I prayed as I groped around to recover my money.

Finally, I managed to get through. Trying to make a poetic joke to lighten the mood, I asked Liz if she had a room somewhere, far away from the cold night air. Luckily, she didn't slam the phone down. Instead, I asked her if she could please come and collect me. I promised I would, in the future, go to any nightclub of her choice. I would even get up and dance. I was that desperate. This time she did slam the phone down, but only after assuring me that she was on her way.

I had to keep moving. Just those few minutes of inactivity had taken their toll. I started to run once more. Ten minutes later, I saw headlights approaching. Around the corner came the family car. I have never been so pleased and grateful to see that old Volvo Estate. The car pulled up next to me, and I struggled to open the door. Liz leaned across and pushed the door open, shouting at me to get in. I think she called me a flaming idiot, although I may have misheard the first word.

I tried to break the ice; I had a lot of that to break, by asking her how her night had gone. I was met with stony silence. Realising that silence was probably the best way to go, I sunk back in my seat and tried not to shiver too much.

"And stop singing that bloody song. It's not funny anymore," she demanded.

I had not even realised that I was still singing it. I apologised once more and sunk even deeper into my seat, trying not to make matters even worse by my silly remarks.

In the end, the only real casualty of that night was my beloved suede boots. They literally fell apart as I prised them from my frozen feet. My credibility had also fallen apart as I was the butt of many jokes amongst our friends for quite some time.

Fast forward five years. My father had left his car in our driveway whilst he went away on holiday. He returned earlier than planned and was very upset that we were not present at home to give him the car keys. Instead of collecting his car, he had to take a taxi home. The journey to Worthing cost him a small fortune and he was not best pleased.

The next day, we arrived back from visiting Liz's family. The message light was blinking away on the answering machine. Pressing play, I was surprised at the angry message left by my father. I called him and apologised for not being home when he turned up, albeit he had arrived earlier than expected. This was a long before any of us had the luxury of a mobile phone. To appease him, I promised to drive his car down to Worthing and then get a train home.

The next day, I duly drove down, taking Jack, our Golden Retriever, with me. The drive was thirty miles, and I arrived punctually at the time I had promised. Knocking on his door, I waited to be thanked for returning the car. Instead of being thanked, I was rebuked for bringing my dog. He told me that getting all the dog hairs out of his car would take him forever. He drove probably one of the worst cars ever produced, the dreadful Triumph Acclaim. At first, I thought he was joking, but when he shouted at my dog, that was enough for me. Jack and I turned around and set off for the railway station.

It was not a long way, about thirty minutes. I walked up to the ticket office and asked for a ticket back home. I inquired if there was an additional charge for my dog. The ticket agent assured me that there were no extra charges for dogs, which I thought was an excellent policy. "We don't charge for dogs as we don't allow dogs" was not the reply I wanted to hear.

And so, here I was again, deja vu! I was standing at a station with no obvious way to get home. This time, I did not have the luxury of being able to call Liz; she was away on a trip.

And so, I bent down and rubbed Jack's ears. As his trusting dark brown eyes looked up at me, I asked him if he fancied a little run. It was either that or leaving him there.

We decided that the run was the more appropriate solution, and so that is precisely what we did. Initially, I tried desperately to get Jack to calm down. He was a young dog and constantly pulled on his lead. He wanted to go as fast as possible. I tried to explain to him that we had thirty miles ahead of us. It made no difference, Jack continued pulling on his lead.

Six hours later, it was a very different Jack that plodded those last few miles. We had set off late in the morning and arrived home early in the evening. It was a lovely day this time, and I was in shorts and had the correct footwear. However, it was still a challenging journey and I must admit that we walked quite a bit of the time. That was Jack's fault, not mine, at least that was what I kept telling myself as I plodded those last few miles.

Chapter 33

Running with the Hounds

Since I started running all those years ago, I have been lucky enough to have owned three Golden Retrievers. I say owned, but I'm not too fond of that terminology. We never felt as though we owned any of our dogs. They were simply part of the family or maybe, they owned us.

My first dog was Roffey, a big bundle of golden fur who loved everyone and everything. I was just beginning my flying career when Roffey came into my life. I was single, living in a flat and teaching other people how to fly. The very first day I bought Roffey, suddenly, and very unexpectedly, I had to go flying. I had a twelve-week-old puppy and had little choice but to take him with me in the two-seater aircraft. Luckily, Roffey loved the experience and continued to fly with me for many years. He ended up on the front page of a local newspaper as a photo was snapped of him apparently taxiing an executive jet onto the stand. The full story is told in my first book, *The Self Improver.*

Because I was so busy flying, Roffey and I usually had little time to go for runs together. When eventually, I met Liz, whom Roffey introduced me to, my career had finally started to calm down. Roffey and I had more time to run together. Some dogs are born to run. Others, like Roffey, will run when they have to, but you can see that their hearts are not really in it. Roffey was one such dog. We would set off, but sooner or later, Roffey would discover a smell so enticing and overpowering that he had to stop to investigate further. These investigations could last moments, but more often than not, they lasted minutes. He would approach the smell from all angles and give it his full attention. He usually repeated the process at least three times before lifting one of his back legs and adding to whatever aroma had gained his attention.

Whilst, of course, I did not mind this, it interrupted my running rhythm. It was a stop-start all the way. Neither of us was particularly satisfied when we got home. However, Roffey could not have disliked it that much. As soon as he saw me in my running gear, he was ready with his nose pushed up against the front door.

Roffey continued running with me until he was nearly fifteen, a good age for a retriever. It was the fact that we stopped so often that allowed Roffey to continue running for such a long period of time. He still loved to walk and did so for the next two years. Eventually, time caught up with him, and he struggled to walk even a few steps. After calling the vet I was asked to bring Roffey in for the final time. I carried him to the car and Roffey and I drove to the surgery.

His favourite thing in the whole world was to have a piece of a Mars bar. He would sell his soul for that chocolate. Outside the surgery, I opened the estate car's rear door and produced three Mars bars. Despite his condition, Roffey wagged his tail and lifted his head to receive these gifts. All three chocolate bars were gone in a flash. I lifted him up and received a lick on the face as a thank you. As I carried him into the surgery, Roffey suddenly became very tense. He had been there many times before and had never shown even the slightest hesitation. I am totally convinced that Roffey knew what was coming. Gently, I lowered him onto the table and stroked his head. There was no tail wagging now. I even produced the fourth Mars bar, which I had been saving to distract him from what was about to happen. He didn't even look at it. Instead, he looked directly into my eyes, as if searching for a reason why I was doing this to him.

A moment later, he was gone, and my heart was broken. I lifted his lifeless body as carefully as possible and carried him back to the car. He had been my best friend for the past seventeen years. We buried him in our large back garden with full canine honours underneath the trees. He was wrapped in his blanket, his head resting on his favourite pillow.

I gently laid that last uneaten Mars bar next to him and added a few of his toys. And with that, we said farewell to our wonderful Roffey. If I could give any dog owner some advice, it would be never, ever take your dog to the vet to be put down. Get the vet to come to you and allow your dog the dignity to pass away in the comfort and security of its own home. Roffey knew why he was at the vet's, and all these years later, it still haunts me that I let him down in his final moments of life. I am so sorry, Roffey. Please forgive me.

Naturally, our two young children were also heartbroken. Roffey had always been part of the family, a huge part of their lives. Without Roffey, life seemed somehow empty. And so, a little sooner than I would have liked, we were the proud owners of another retriever puppy. Jack had arrived.

We saw an advertisement in a local paper. A family had bought a Golden Retriever puppy. Unfortunately, their other dog would not accept him. One dog had to go and fortunately for us, it was the new puppy. Jack was sixteen weeks old, still a puppy but a very large one. Jack continued this growth spurt and ended up becoming a very large dog indeed.

Unlike Roffey, Jack loved to run. He was born to run. He was never happier than when he was running. There was only one problem. He didn't like running with me. Instead, he loved to run away from me. Please do not get me wrong. Jack was a very loving, kind and gentle dog. Indoors, he was perfect. On a lead, he was great. However, the moment he was left to his own devices, he was off.

We would go for a run in the woods. Jack would run by my side, and all seemed well with the world. And then, Jack would get a scent of a deer, fox, badger, or whatever creature took his fancy. It was like he had a switch in his brain between a great dog and a bad dog. You never knew when he would throw that switch. Once he was gone, he was well and truly gone. I grew to recognise the signs when he was ready to leave me alone in the woods. His ears would prick up, and his nose would start to twitch. At that point, I would make a grab for his collar. If I missed, he could be gone for hours or even days. He was that naughty. Of course, I tried running with him on a lead, but it did not work. All dogs like to stop and sniff and cock their legs. This meant I was continually stopping and starting, which was highly unsatisfactory for a runner.

Jack did not restrict his great escaping act to just when we were running. If you opened the back door, he thought of himself as Houdini and perform a vanishing act. He would wander into the garden and then suddenly, run as fast as he could into the surrounding woodland. We have a large garden, more than enough for a dog to run and enjoy himself. This, however, was not enough for Jack. He would jump over hedges and fences to gain his freedom.

We were at our wits' end. It was getting ridiculous. We constantly had people ringing us to let us know that they had found Jack. Eventually, I fitted an electrical collar on him when he went into the garden. I spent days laying a cable around the garden's perimeter, a time-consuming and costly exercise.

The idea was that when Jack approached the cable, his collar would start to buzz and beep. This was meant to deter him from getting any closer to the hedges. If he continued towards the boundary, the collar would increase the buzzing and beeping. Within a few feet, it would produce quite a significant electric shock. I hated fitting this to Jack. It was cruel and unkind. However, it was better than losing him. He could run for miles and be oblivious to roads and traffic whilst in pursuit of whatever he was chasing. Sooner or later, he would get run over or cause a traffic accident.

At first, the collar worked well. Jack would approach whichever hedge he intended to run through or jump over. The collar buzzed away and produced the shock designed to make him move back, away from the boundary. I sat there watching Jack. He was a clever dog. He knew that he was going to get a shock if he got too close to the hedge and he moved away, problem solved.

And then he worked out how to overcome this problem. Instead of walking up to the fence, he ran at it as fast as he could. He then leapt through the air, passing over the vicinity of the hidden cable at full pelt. He got a shock, but only for the briefest of moments. The pain was obviously worth it to escape the confines of our garden. Apparently, the same pain was not worth it when eventually, he decided it was time to come home. We would hear him crying pitifully to be let back into the garden. So basically, we had spent hundreds of pounds on a system that kept our dog out of the garden, not in it.

The situation got worse and worse. Almost every week, we received phone calls from people who had found Jack. Sometimes, they were up to five miles away. Boy, that dog could really run. And then, the inevitable happened, Jack was hit by a passing car as he chased a fox. Unfortunately, I was away, so Liz had to deal with the aftermath alone. Jack had escaped from the garden yet again and chased a fox straight across the road in front of our house. The car hit him full-on. Luckily, the driver was not hurt, and there was no damage to his vehicle. The same, sadly, could not be said for Jack. He was rushed to the vet, where immediately, he was operated on. His injuries were bad but fortunately not life-threatening. Incredibly, he made a full recovery. Even more remarkably, he seemed to have finally learned his lesson. He never ran away again. Talk about having some sense knocked into you. It was a hell of a costly way for him to learn his lesson.

Jack was now ten years old. For the first nine, he had been a very naughty boy. At times, we were at our wits' end. We spent more time jumping in the car to go and fetch him back than we did walking him. That had all changed. He was now in what I called his 'golden years'. Sadly his age meant that we could no longer run long distances together. We had a routine. I would take him for a twenty-minute run and return to the car. He would jump in and settle down whilst I went for another run. This was an ideal compromise for both of, although unfortunately, it was not too last for long.

Jack began to struggle to keep up even on a short run. I could see that he was doing his best, but he was really struggling. I stopped running with him, we just walked instead. When even this seemed beyond him, we took him back to the vet. After a brief examination, we were told that Jack had a small lump close to the area where he had been hit the previous year. It was probably just scar tissue but should be removed to be on the safe side. Wholly reassured, we patted Jack on his head and told him we would pick him up later that afternoon.

I was alone when my mobile phone rang a few hours later. It was the vet. She had Jack on the operating table and had stepped out to call me. It was not scar tissue; poor Jack was riddled with cancer. The vet advised me that it would be cruel to bring Jack back. She strongly recommended letting him go peacefully whilst under anaesthesia rather than go through the pain of recovery only to be put to sleep in a few days.

I had to make an instant decision, yes or no. I still do not know if I made the right decision. I had no one to ask. Jack passed away peacefully on the operating table. We never had the chance to say a final goodbye to him. I drove to the vet to pick up Jack's body. He is buried under the same tree as Roffey.

I spoke with the vet who had performed the operation. She was amazed that Jack could still walk, such was the extent of his cancer. He must have been in severe pain for many weeks, yet he never showed it. In that last year, I believe he did his best to make up for all the times he had let us down. The vet speculated that the car accident was probably the catalyst for cancer. And so Jack's antics were almost certainly why we lost him at a relatively young age. Looking back now, I am grateful that we had our golden years together, saddened that we never had the chance to say goodbye. Sleep well, Jacky boy.

After this episode, we decided we needed a break from the heartache of owning a dog. The thought of losing another dog was just too painful. We needed time away from the responsibility and commitment of owning a dog. The freedom of being able to travel without worrying about dog care seemed really appealing. No more dog hairs, no more muddy paws. I could sell my old estate car, which was more of a mobile kennel, and buy myself something small and sporty. There were so many reasons not to get another dog. And that was why nine months after we lost Jack, the four of us were driving up the motorway to see another puppy.

Chapter 34

My Four-Legged Friend

This book starts with a dedication to Alfie. In fact, this entire book is dedicated to the most unique running partner anyone could possibly wish for. And to think that in the beginning, I didn't even want him.

Our two previous retrievers had been big dogs, especially Jack, who was the size of a large Alsatian. They were known as show retrievers, not that I knew that at the time we had them. We only discovered that there were different types of Golden Retrievers when we went to see Alfie. Apparently, he was a working retriever. That sounded good to me. Maybe, he would pay his own way in life.

Alfie was born eight weeks before we first met him in Bicester, a two-hour drive from where we lived. The boys were keen to get another dog. I was not so sure. Maybe, it was still too soon after losing Jack. I was persuaded that it couldn't hurt to go and see the litter. And so, the four of us set off to do battle with the dreaded M25 motorway as if I didn't do that enough going to work!

We arrived at a very impressive manor house set on its own grounds. There was a scruffy-looking little dog at the front chasing stones. 'Obviously not the brightest of creatures', I thought to myself, as tennis balls were sitting idly by. The lovely lady who lived there pointed to this small brown dog and proudly introduced her as the mother of the litter. Well, that was enough for me. I was ready to turn around and drive home. What a waste of a journey. That was definitely not a retriever; it was far too small and obviously as daft as a box of frogs. If she were anything to go by, her puppies would not have much going for them.

We were taken to the back of the farmhouse, where seven little puppies were running around, jumping over each other and generally having a great time. I had to admit that they looked adorable, but they still did not look like any retriever I had ever seen.

I had had enough and was more than ready to leave. Rob, however, had a different idea. He stepped into the dog pen and sat down. It was only at this point that we realised there were, in fact, eight puppies, not seven. The first seven ran to Rob, rolled all over him and then set off to play in another part of the enclosure. One puppy had sat watching the commotion, not joining in, just watching. Once his siblings had finished exploring Rob, this little puppy stood up, walked over to where Rob was sitting cross-legged. He then climbed into his lap. The puppy then looked up into Rob's face and as he bent down, the puppy gently licked his face. Well, that was that, as far as the family was concerned, they had found our new dog. I, on the other hand, was not convinced. I kept thinking back to the mother and her obsession with fetching stones.

I asked to see the father, and that, for me, was where the decision was finally made. Apparently, the father had died of cancer a few weeks previously. 'No', I thought to myself, 'we had just lost our dog to cancer'. There was no way I could go through that again.

Thanking the breeder, I rounded up the family, herded them into the car and drove away. And that should have been the end of that. Of course, it wasn't. I was totally outnumbered. Everyone wanted this puppy apart from me. I still thought he was not really a retriever at all, although I must admit that the pictures we were shown of his father revealed a very handsome dog.

The following week we were back on the M25 to have another look at this little puppy. We were met by the same lady who informed us that all but one of the puppies had now either been bought or had been reserved. Three pairs of accusing eyes bore into me. I was certainly not Mr Popular. Again, we were taken to the rear of the house and left alone. Sure enough, there were now only four puppies in the enclosure. I felt terribly guilty. Why, oh, why had I been such a stubborn fool the previous week?

Rob again sat in the pen; the remaining puppies ignored him this time. They were too busy playing with each other. Rob stood up and left the puppies to their games. It was time to go home. Even I, who didn't want a puppy, felt despondent. Rob had really fallen for that puppy, as had Liz and James. It was all my fault. that he had gone to another home.

And then, we heard a tiny yelp. I saw a little puppy sitting alone in a separate pen. He recognised Rob, and Rob recognised him. He stepped into the pen and sat down. The puppy climbed onto his lap, and just as he had done a week earlier, he gently licked Rob's face. It looked as though we had a new dog, after all.

Suddenly, it occurred to me that this puppy had probably been put into a separate area as he had been reserved or sold.

This choice had a one-in-five chance of going horribly wrong. The tension was broken when the breeder returned and explained that this little pup had been isolated as his siblings were bullying him. Also, he was the only puppy still for sale. Nobody else had wanted him. He had sat alone when potential buyers came to view the litter. Not once had he approached anyone since we had visited last week. Immediately, we knew why this was. He was waiting for Rob to come back and take him home.

Alfie came with us to his new home that very afternoon. I had driven there, so Liz drove home. I sat in the back just in case our new puppy became distressed at leaving his siblings. He was snuggled up with the boys and looked as though he had never been happier, which, to be fair, he probably hadn't. Feeling slightly jealous and left out, I lifted the puppy onto my chest. He promptly threw up right into my mouth. My relationship with Alfie had yet to get off to a good start. I was assured that it was just Alfie's way of telling me off for nearly losing him. They were right. He never did it again.

Alfie grew from a skinny little puppy into the most beautiful dog you could wish for. He was simply stunning. We could not take him anywhere without being stopped and asked where we had got him from or if they could stroke him. He entered and won a dog beauty competition. The professional photographer who took the picture twelve years ago, still has that picture on his studio wall, and Alfie's photo still gets compliments which is nice to know.

Nine months after he had arrived, I took Alfie out for his first run. I was very nervous. Would he enjoy running with me? Like almost every dog he loved running, but that is very different from running with someone.

Many dogs simply do not want to run with their owners. They want to run alone. Roffey was like that. I had no idea if Jack liked it or not. He was never there long enough to find out.

With heart in mouth, I set off, hoping Alfie would follow me. He sat by the car and watched me with a quizzical look on his face. I could see him wondering why I was running away from him instead of walking with him. And then, the penny dropped, and he jumped up and ran after me. He actually ran after me and not away from me. I was so happy that I could have cried. Alfie stayed with me for the whole run, not once moving more than a few feet from my side. I would allow him to do his business before we set off and again when we finished our run. He never once let me down in the years we ran together. I could literally trust him with my life.

As he got older, he could run even faster and further. He loved every moment. He would look at me as I struggled to keep up with him and wonder why I was so slow. But he would always wait for me, somehow understanding that I was not his equal. He would look at me with those huge, soft, brown eyes and somehow, innately understood that he had to adjust his pace and make allowances for me.

As the years slipped past, the roles began to reverse slowly, very slowly. As Alf aged, he was not the one always up ahead. For a while, we were equals. We both ran at the same pace for the same distance. And then, I realised that it was me who was looking back at Alf, willing him to run a little faster for a little longer. I could see in Alf's eyes that he could not understand why this was happening to us.

For ten happy years, Alfie and I ran every day I was home. We had many adventures together. It was so liberating to run with a dog you knew would be there at the end of the run. Liz and I took him on staycations. Everywhere we went, Alfie came along. If it meant staying in poorer-quality hotels, as they were the only ones that accepted dogs, then that's where we stayed. Alfie never went to kennels. Instead, he only stayed with friends who we knew and trusted. He was never spoiled, but we treated him as one of the family, which of course, he was.

We took him on a surfing holiday in Newquay in Cornwall. Alf watched as I dragged my board into the waves, climbed on and surfed back to the beach. Alf wanted to have a go, and so he did. I hired a giant, stable, foam beginners board and gave Alf his first and only lesson. Unlike me, he only needed to be shown something once. Eventually, he would hold the surfboard's rope in his mouth and swim out to where everyone else was waiting for a wave. He would clamber onto the board and wait for the surf to take him back in. He would repeat this until we had both exhausted ourselves. We would then both go for a beer.

Another time, we were swimming together when a pod of dolphins came into the bay. The dolphins surrounded us, and not knowing how they would react, and to be safe, I held Alfie tightly against my chest. I was just within my depth. Alfie relaxed in my arms, perfectly content and trusting that I could deal with any potential danger. The lifeguard launched a boat to come to our aid. There was no need. The dolphins looked at Alfie; Alfie looked back at the dolphins. Both decided neither constituted a threat, and the dolphins swam majestically away. 'Did that really happen?' I thought to myself, as a very worried-looking lifeguard asked if we were okay. Totally unconcerned, Alfie swam back to the shore, unaware of the crowd that had gathered to watch him. He looked very pleased with himself as the crowd clapped as he stood shaking himself dry.

The runs with Alf were the best runs that I have ever had. Sharing things with a dog is so rewarding, and Alf and I were having the time of our lives, and then, suddenly, everything changed.

Alfie had never been that interested in food. We would fill his bowl each morning and evening. He would nibble away, walk away and then, eventually, finish his meal. We tried various dog foods, but none seemed to interest him greatly. And then we tried frozen, fresh, raw meat. This really seemed to tickle Alfie's fancy, and he wolfed it down.

For the next year, we fed him what we believed was the healthiest dog food available. Slowly, we noticed a change in his toilet habits. He seemed to be having trouble emptying his bowels. Eventually, we took him to the vet with a feeling of dread. 'Here we go again', I thought to myself. The diagnosis was not good. Alf had a severe blockage in his lower bowel. Despite trying everything to eradicate the blockage, it was finally decided that an operation was the only option. Alf was taken in, and a large section of his bowel was removed. It turned out that we had inadvertently been slowly killing our dog. The raw meat we were feeding him had a large amount of ground-up bone mixed in with the meat. This had built up in his bowel over time, causing the blockage. Alf stayed at the surgery that night, and I went to pick him up the next afternoon.

I was sitting in a crowded waiting room when a nurse brought Alf out. She walked towards me with a very unsteady Alf at her side. Suddenly, Alf saw me. He then let out the most blood-curdling howl that I have ever heard. The nurse was so shocked that she dropped his lead. Everyone and every animal just froze and stared at Alf. For his part, Alf leapt into my lap and shook like a leaf. It took me at least two minutes to calm him and stop him from crying.

Unfortunately, he had torn the stitches holding his wound together with that leap. The vet wanted to keep him in for another night to restitch his injury. I refused, instead I carried Alf back into the consulting room. Once there I gently put him on the examination table and asked her to do it there and then. I could then take him straight home. The vet was very hesitant, afraid that Alfie was too weak for anymore anaesthetics. I asked her to repair the torn stitches, Alf would be fine without any more drugs. As she stitched him, Alf just stood there, suffering the pain without uttering a sound. He seemed to know that as long as I was there, he would be going home that day.

Alfie never really recovered from that operation. From that day onwards, he had trouble with his bowels. He spent the remainder of his life on a cocktail of drugs. We changed vets and found the wonderful Alex, who finally seemed to understand the problem and how to care for Alfie. He and I never ran together again. He was still not an old dog, he was only ten, but the operation had aged him. He still loved life and could walk for miles. He just could not run. I was back to running by myself. It hurt so much that I had lost my best running partner, and it still does.

Alfie persevered, coping well with all the medications he had to endure. On bad nights, he would have to wake us up seven times every night. He would rush outside to relieve himself and return, looking upset and drained. Wiping his usually muddy feet, we would return to bed only to repeat the whole process an hour later. On good nights, he would only have us up once or twice. Despite all of this, Alf still enjoyed his life. He loved to swim, walk and help me write books.

We took Alf to Bath for a visit to my sister-in-law, Karen. It was a three-hour drive, and we arrived late in the afternoon. I had forgotten to bring a jacket, and the forecast was for rain. We left Alf with Karen and went into town to buy me a coat. He was pretty relaxed to see us go. He knew Karen and knew we would soon be back. We were only away for an hour, and when we returned, he was his usual happy self.

The following day we took Alf for a walk. Again, he was his usual lovely self. We decided to visit the Roman Baths and leave Alfie with Karen. The three of us got into Karen's car; the plan was for her to drop us off, and we would get the bus back. There was no room in the car for Alf.

Before we set off, I realised I had forgotten my new jacket. I jumped out of the car and let myself back into the house. Alfie came to the door and asked again if he could come along with us. My return, after saying goodbye, gave him fresh hope that I had changed my mind. I patted him on the head and told him I would see him very soon. With that, I closed the door and left him alone. That was to be the last time I ever saw Alfie alive.

Two hours later, Karen called Liz and said that Alfie had been sick. He occasionally did this, and we told her not to worry. Half an hour later, she rang again. Alfie had been sick again, and he was crying. That most definitely was not normal.

Immediately, we left the Roman Baths and tried to find a taxi, but there were none to be seen. I felt in my new jacket for my phone to use my Uber app. For the first time ever, I had forgotten my phone. Today of all days, I had no way of calling an Uber. We waited for nearly forty minutes before a bus came along. Twenty minutes later, we jumped off the bus and ran to Karen's door. We were beside ourselves with worry. Karen opened the door with a big smile on her face. She assured us Alfie was much better. He had stopped crying and was asleep under the table.

Relief flooded through us as we went to see our beloved dog. As we looked at Alfie lying there, we both instantly knew that Alfie was not asleep. He was dead.

Liz let out a howl, the memory of which still chills me to the bone. She fell onto her knees and sobbed. I bent down and buried my face in his beautiful, warm furry neck. We had missed him by minutes. Had I remembered my phone, we would have been there when he died. Instead, he died alone, crying out for his family. Karen was distraught; She had no idea that Alf had passed away.

As gently as possible, I lifted Alfie into my arms and carried him to our Land Rover. Liz had put his bed in the boot, where he had spent so much time going places with us and loved to be. We gently laid him in his bed and covered him with his blanket. That drive home was the worst journey I have ever made. I sobbed and sobbed, the tears making driving difficult at times.

Rob set off from his home in London to meet us as we got home. We decided to bury Alfie under the same bush where he sat on his first day with us. It is a beautiful Acer shrub which rewards us with an incredible display of colour each year. It

seems the perfect place for our perfect friend, Alfie, to rest.
Every day, I stop on my run at the place where Alf liked to sniff.
I remind him of just how much he was loved and how much we
will always miss him. I hope the acer, beneath which he is
buried, will look after him as well as we did.

Chapter 35

You Don't Have to be Mad to Run ...

We should all be more aware of mental health issues and their consequences. Like everyone who has drawn breath, I have had my fair share of downs. It is how we cope that is the crucial thing.

The last thing you probably want to hear as your plane hurtles down the runway is that your pilot is depressed, generally fed up, or feeling like giving up. Pilots are just as likely to suffer from depression, anxiety, or mental health problems as anyone else. In a recent survey, being an airline pilot was the third most stressful job after firefighters and policemen. The main difference is that a depressed firefighter or police officer may endanger their colleagues or the public. An airline pilot with depression can be the cause of a major catastrophe.

This is now a serious concern for the airlines and the travelling public. The job has changed dramatically since I first began to fly. What other job starts the day with security guards, X-raying your possessions, then pulling everything out of your flight bag and then sniffing your breath to detect any sign that you had one too many drinks the previous night? Pilots are the most scanned people on earth. It's a miracle that we do not glow in the dark.

Having been humiliated in front of our passengers, we now have to spend up to sixteen hours locked away in a small 'office'. We only leave the flight deck for essential reasons. We then spend days in a third-rate hotel before repeating the process all over again.

Airline management gets rewarded for driving down the lifestyles of their pilots whilst driving up the number of hours they have to fly. It has become a race to the bottom that we pilots can never win. Once these managers have squeezed every last ounce from their pilot workforce, they take a huge bonus from the savings made and then move on to another company or industry. They may have only worked for an airline for a few years, but the damage they can inflict on a pilot's mental health through cost-cutting decisions will last for the remainder of their career. Due to the seniority system, airline pilots usually stay with their airline for most of their careers. They see these managers come, wreak havoc, and then leave. It is incredibly frustrating and depressing having to constantly fight to keep yourself and everyone who flies with you safe from these draconian executives.

I remember clearly when one such manager proposed that we fly to the East Coast of America three times in succession without a day off to recover. I challenged him that this was probably the most stupid and most dangerous thing I had ever heard. In reply to my complaint, he declared that he would accompany me on my next New York flight to assess just how tiring the flight was.

Sure enough, this manager walked straight into the flight deck on my next flight and announced his presence. He interrupted our crucial safety briefing and started talking about money-saving ideas. Slowly, I turned around and asked him politely if he had ever walked into anyone else's office and interrupted a meeting. He needed to understand that we were busy discussing our departure route and any emergencies we may face. It was only when I pointed to the door and asked him to use it that the penny finally dropped. Then, he informed me that he was the senior manager and that he, and only he, would decide when the time to leave had arrived.

Luckily, he had not checked in any luggage, as we would have been even more delayed as security marched him off the aircraft. Unbelievably, he then wrote an article proclaiming that he had flown to the East Coast three times in a row and had not felt fatigued. That he had slept in First Class on all three flights probably had something to do with it.

You may be wondering what a book about running has to do with all of this. Running was one of the best ways to deal with these, at times, overwhelming pressures.

Being a pilot is an excellent career choice that most people would envy. However, it is stressful, and everyone needs a way to cope. My choice was to go for a run. It is incredible how quickly life's everyday problems become less significant the further you run. Personal and work frustrations seem less overwhelming as you grunt your way up a steep hill or gaze out over a lake. The only other time that I have felt such an almost surreal benefit was walking in the Grand Canyon. The Canyon's sheer size and beauty make your problems seem trivial and unimportant. Just stand there and look around you. How can our problems matter that much in the greater scheme of things? If you ever get the chance to go there, please do. It may also be cheaper than therapy.

Running is also the time to clear your mind of the clutter and white noise of everyday living. This is especially true when running in nature's woodlands or other remote places. After every such run, I feel the stress and strains literally leave my body, and I am ready to cope with whatever life or a stupid manager can throw at me.

Chapter 36

Advice From an Old, Sometimes Bold, Runner

I started running in the 1960s and it's been a long journey to get to this point. Hopefully, there are still many more miles to cover before I hang up my running gear, or I run out of luck when pointing to my shoes in a desperate attempt to get away from an adversary.

I have never broken any records, nor will I, unless it's for the longest running career. None of my runs has been outstanding in any sense of the word. I have simply put one foot in front of the other and waited to see where destiny and my size twelve feet would take me.

My one and only claim to fame is that I tend to do things for a longer time than others. I flew the Boeing 747 for a record-breaking thirty-four years. Nobody else has spent more time flying what, to me, was the aircraft that changed the way we all fly.

My running career has progressed along similar lines. I have continued running through the decades without quite realising that this was unusual. Since the early 1980s, I have run at least five kilometres every single day. Naturally, I missed the odd day through sickness, injury or work. However, if I missed a day, I would run twice as far the next day to make up for it. Often, I would run for eight or ten kilometres, sometimes a lot more. At one point, I had become the Forrest Gump of the pilot world. If you add up my daily distance, I run a marathon a week, that's every week, fifty-two weeks a year. Yet, I do this at my own pace, in my own time, and I still love it.

I read in awe of people who run ultra-marathons, triathlons, iron men competitions, and one hundred marathons in one hundred days. These are the real superstars of the running world; I am a simple amateur who enjoys my beer as much as I do my running. I pound the streets of the world with the simple aim of getting back to where I started. This is not always as simple as it sounds, as I hope I have demonstrated.

If this book has inspired or even started you to think about running, may I offer some advice? I am a great believer that it is better to learn from other people's mistakes rather than your own.

Many people start to run before getting in shape to run. Now, that may sound a little back to front, but please bear with me. If you have been inactive for many years, then you almost certainly are not ready to go for a run. Think of running as your end goal, not your starting point. So many people commit to fitness and think running is a great place to start, but believe me, it isn't! If you pull on a pair of old trainers, shorts that last saw the light of day twenty years ago and a badly fitting top, you are almost doomed to failure. After five or ten minutes, your lunch will be in your mouth; your ears will be filled with the sound of your own heart beating; your feet will be developing painful blisters that will burst a few hours later; and you will stop running, walk home and put your running stuff away for another twenty years.

There are many great books about running written by people far more qualified than myself to give advice. Look up the *Couch to 5K* programme on the internet. It's all great stuff with excellent advice. Yet somehow, these publications seem to either overlook or skim over the fact that to start running is tough. I see advertisements on the television of someone on a settee eating cake and crisps and then competing in park runs a few weeks later. Do not be fooled. Life is never that easy.

If you really want to make a difference in your life and running forms part of that change, then take things literally, step by step. Buy a new pair of trainers and don't buy the cheapest ones you can find. Equally, do not go for the newest, most expensive designer pair of trainers; these can be equally as useless. Buy a middle-of-the-road, excuse the pun, decent pair of running shoes. They will not break the bank, but they may well stop you from breaking something even more painful. There is nothing more important to a runner than the shoes they wear. Even today, if I do not have my running shoes with me, I simply will not go for a run. I will do more harm than good by trying to run in anything but my trusted running shoes. Stupidly, I did my thirty-mile Brighton run in a pair of suede boots, but that was under the influence of a few beers, and my feet hurt like hell for a few days!

Once equipped with this vital asset, you are ready to start getting ready to run. It does not matter much what clothes you wear, just make sure that they are comfortable and suitable for the weather outside. This may seem obvious, but over the decades, I have seen runners struggle with too much clothing in the summer and too little in the winter. Unbelievably, I may have been guilty of that in the past so you can learn from my mistakes.

Depending on your starting point, decide on a walk that will raise your heart rate just a little but make sure that your heart knows about what your body is doing. Again, I have no medical qualifications whatsoever. If you need to check with your doctor before starting any exercise programme, then it is essential that you do so.

After your first walk, power walk, or whichever walk you choose, you should feel that you have had some exercise. At no point should you be out of breath but breathing heavily is a good sign that you have achieved your goal for the day.

From there on, it is simply a matter of a little further, a little faster, with each walk. Try putting on a backpack and walking uphill. That is still something I do when recovering from an injury or illness. It's all about getting ready to run.

Allow yourself at least two weeks of walking before attempting the next stage. Remember, this is a lifestyle change that you want to last a lifetime. It is not a race. If you need longer in the walking phase, take that as a sign that you're not ready and enjoy it. Another great tip is to buy a fitness tracker. Again, you do not need anything fancy, just a basic tracker to measure how far and how long you have moved. If you can afford one that measures your heart rate at the same time, even better. You can now really see your progress as these gadgets do not lie, and it can be incredibly satisfying to see your improvement. Nothing motivates better than progress.

You will know when it is time to add a little jogging to your walks. Pick a tree or lamppost up ahead and break into a gentle jog until you reach your goal. Don't try to carry on until the next marker. That's not the point. You are trying to explore your recovery rate, the time it takes your body to recover from strenuous exercise. The shorter the recovery time, the fitter you are.

If you felt fine after this jog on that walk, try it again on your next walk. Just jog a little longer on each subsequent outing. Again do this walk/jog/walk routine for at least two weeks. Please do not be tempted to shorten this phase. Remember, once again that you are in this for the long haul.

A month after starting, you could now be ready to start running. Once again, everyone is different, and it may take you considerably longer to get to this point. It really does not matter how long it takes you to get there. It's getting there that matters.

When I was teaching new students to fly, there seemed to be the concept that you should be ready to go on your first solo flight after twelve hours of instruction. This is totally untrue, and some of the best students I ever taught took considerably longer than twelve hours. These pilots carried on to become training captains with some of the world's best airlines. Had they become discouraged after passing the twelve-hour mark, the world of aviation would have been a poorer place.

Start your runs gently. Replace the walk/run/walk routine with a run/walk/run one. Choose a point to stop and then start to run again. Never get to the point where you are so out of breath that you cannot speak. Leave that to when you go running in São Paulo! From this point onwards, reduce the number of times you stop running until you can run the whole way. You are now a runner. Welcome to my world!

Where you go from here is entirely up to you. My only remaining piece of advice is not to push yourself too hard too quickly. It is far better for your health to run little and often than to attempt a long-distance run that could result in injury or you giving up running. Treat your new, not too expensive, running shoes as friends that you want to see often but for not too long. That way, you will remain friends, until it's time to replace your shoes, not put them in a cupboard for the next twenty years.

Epilogue

Running Away from Old Age

I have always had one eye over my shoulder on every run that I have ever done. In my youth, I saw nothing but the route I had just run along. As I approached middle age, I could see a faint shadow on the pavement behind me, nothing that I could identify, but a shadow, nevertheless. In middle age, I found myself checking more and more to see what or who was following me. This shadow was getting larger and more pronounced.

In my fifties, I could now hear footsteps. They were getting closer with every run. The spectre was beginning to take on a more sinister form.

I am currently in my mid-sixties. There is no need to look behind me on every run. Instead, I can look in front and see the shadow of old Father Time. He is now so close to my shoulder that his shadow is beginning to overtake me. I try hard to accelerate away, sometimes it works, and his shadow recedes. On other days, I feel my age. My legs ache, and old injuries plague me. Still, I push ahead, and eventually, the shadow diminishes once more.

Years ago, this would have depressed me. Today, I smile at the spectre of Old Father Time. Why shouldn't I? I am still ahead and have no intention of letting him overtake me quite yet. My game plan is to run until my body demands that I stop. I don't know when this will be, but I rarely listen to my body, so it will hopefully be a long time from now.

I have been so fortunate to have been able to combine my flying career with my passion for running. Yes, of course, my runs have taken me into places that are best avoided but to know the areas to avoid, you have to experience them first.

I have met real danger, the mob in Lagos, the muggers in Jamaica and the would-be assailants in Sao Paulo.

However, the most chilling and scary moment in all of my runs was the look my wife gave me when I missed that pre-wedding lunch. It can still keep me awake at night. I absolutely maintain that they were giant rats. The next time we visit the castle in Italy, I may do that same run just to check.

Surely I could not be that stupid, or could I?

Run Safe,

Nick Eades

About the Author

Author Nick Eades is originally from the South coast of England where he grew up in a family with a strong aviation background, close to Shoreham Airport in Sussex.

Nick had a very successful career as an airline pilot. Initially, he self-trained, a story told in his first book, *The Self-Improver*.

He then went on to spend thirty-four years with British Airways during which time he created the world record as a pilot flying the Boeing 747, a story he tells in his second book, *Still Improving*.

He is now retired and lives in East Grinstead with his wife Liz. They have two grown sons, James and Robert.

Overtaken by a Butterfly is Nick's third book.

Other books by Nick Eades

The Self-Improver: A Pilot's Journey

Still Improving: Becoming the World's Most Experienced 747 Captain

Acknowledgements

Once again, 'life comes at you quickly and memories fade slowly'.

This is my third and last book covering my life story. This book combines my love of aviation and running. I can honestly say that I could not have succeeded in one without the other. Both have brought me happiness, excitement, laughter and the occasional moments of sheer terror.

Of course, without the help and support of my incredible family, Liz and our two boys, James and Rob, none of these things would have any true meaning.

Once again, my thanks go to my publisher, Lionel Ross and my editor, Mark Cripps. Without their help and guidance, my books would have remained a dream, not a reality.

Again, thanks must also go to Sally Pitiakoydis who diligently corrected my many grammatical errors.